A HAND IN THE BUSH
The Fine Art of Vaginal Fisting

A HAND IN THE BUSH
The Fine Art of Vaginal Fisting

Deborah Addington

illustrated by

Megan Rothrock and Jill McCutcheon

Greenery
Press

Cover and interior design: DesignTribe, San Francisco
Cover photograph: MichaelAdrienne
Cover model: Morgana

Published in the United States by Greenery Press, 3739 Balboa Ave. #195, San Francisco, CA 94121.

E-mail: verdant@crl.com

http://www.bigrock.com/~greenery

ISBN 0-890159-02-6

WHAT'S
Inside

ACKNOWLEDGMENTS

This is my first book. It took thirty-two years and innumerable events to get me to this point. With that in mind, I thank you in advance for reading my list of thanks (which reads like a starlet's speech at her first academy awards).

This book and its author owe a great debt and thanks to those who aided in its conception, those who nurtured it, and those who birthed it. I speak for myself, and the pages herein, when I say thank you to Jay Wiseman (conception, with a *man* in the *front* seat of a *moving* vehicle, no less!), Janet, Derek, Francesca and the staff of Greenery Press (labor pains & birth processes). I also wish to offer my love and thanks to my boy, ed, for all of his technical and labor-intensive work; he is my left brain in a right-brained world. To my research assistants – KT, Carol, Janet, and lube boy extraordinaire (Tom!), I offer up my orgasmic gratitude, and an open-ended invitation to do research with me *any* time. It's not that I couldn't have done it without you, my loves, but I'm thoroughly delighted that I didn't have to.

My thanks to my beloved faun, Jain d'Eaux, Dossie Easton, Catherine A. Lizst, Derek, Lynne G., Yew, KT, Kat, weelz[TT], SilvrDrgn, MJ Matson, Jaymes Easton, Susan S., Connie Meredith, and all of the wonderful people who gave me their words;

Thanks to my cat, Chicken (who says she can't wait to read this book), for giving me invaluable assistance with holding down stray pages of manuscript and leaving me cryptic messages written in cat hair on all my black clothing;

Beaucoup de kudos to my fabulous, remarkable, and divinely talented illustrators, Megan and Jill, for turning sow's ears into silk purses and for saving my ass so close to deadline;

Thanks to the doctors who helped clarify the medical issues in this manuscript for me – Beth Brown, M.D., C.C. Chase, M.D., and special gratitude to Charles Moser, Ph.D., M.D., for his consultation, time and knowledge, and this lovely quote about fisting: "Cut your nails, lay back, spread your legs wide, relax and enjoy!"

Thanks to my hairdresser, Rachel, for damage control when I started pulling my hair out by the roots;

A special, loving thank you to my Mom, who will never read farther than this page (don't worry, Mom – if someone you know sees this, they're not bloody likely to tell you);

Many, many thanks to my loving family, especially Watz & Ed & Terra & Alicia, who help to make my world a very interesting place in which to live and write, and a significant and hearty thanks to my sweet, darling, patient, long-suffering, courageous elisabeth, without whose love and support this book would never have gotten past the I'm-thinking-about-writing-a-book stage.

A huge thanks to the women of Tuesday nights and our cheerleaders, for giving me a social life and something to look forward to: Nikki (cow him, Dorothy, you Stonewall homo!), Rosa (I have an idea!), Jacquie, Susan, Sherita (it's all good), Terri (Studd!), Denise, Sarah, Anetra (the perfect cheer), Callahan, Diane, Tina and Meg;

This book is mostly dedicated to Eleni Kali Cozyris, a remarkable woman and lover, whose presence and adventurous spirit helped make me who I am today.

Whatever dedication is left over from Kali goes to renea keesling, who walked with me a crucial part of the path that brought me to this destination; she could contain my fist, even if she couldn't hold my heart.

My deepest thanks to all of you, and my love to all but the last.

Deborah Addington
March, 1997

ABOUT THE AUTHOR

WHO THE
hell is this Addington woman, and why should I listen to her?

Because she has a college degree (which amounts to one really expensive piece of spare toilet paper should she run out of the cheaper stuff), and because she absolutely *loves* to fuck; because she has a cunt, and knows a lot about them. Because she has a fist, and knows a lot about them, too, and because she's smart, funny, and did extensive research at her own expense for this book.

I'm a cunning linguist. I call myself a tribador: I sing of the joys of cunt, and of the ways to make them sing. This book is just one voice in the chorus; it is my wish that you become able, with the help of this score, to expand your range, and add your singing to the chorale of cunty pleasures.

PREFACE

It has been said that "a bird in the hand is worth two in the bush." Anyone who has ever experienced fisting, either as a *fister* or a *fistee*, will probably be happy to tell you that grappling with a wild bird or putting your hand in a bush is pretty much a waste of time, and a lot less sexually gratifying than fisting. I wholeheartedly agree. I call vaginal fisting a "Fine Art" because it requires not only an artistic inclination, but skill and knowledge as well as talent. For some of you, Dear Readers, there will be information within this text that echoes things you may already know. I humbly request that you consider that information a review; feel free to nod wisely in accord while you read on.

Vaginal fisting, also known as *fist-fucking* or *handballing*, is one of those sexual practices that still carries with it a taboo, one born of ignorance. One school of thought has it that the stronger the taboo, the more pleasurable must be the act. In the case of fisting, this is definitely so. Fisting is an incredible experience, not only physically, but mentally and emotionally. It may well be that the taboo helps make fisting as potent an act as it is; then again, it may be that the potency is the reason for the taboo.

When I started doing textual research for this book, I was truly surprised to find out how little written material there is on the subject. Fisting is perhaps my favorite sexual activity; I love its passion and intensity, so I assumed that others would find it appealing and significant. I took it for granted that others thought about it and practiced it as much as I do. That assumption was not supported by the literature I was able to find. I found a few books that had brief sections on vaginal fisting, most of them differing wildly in opinions and "facts."

This subject is not widely discussed over tea or Chablis (hence the writing of this book). That ignorance, that unavailability of information, keeps us from plumbing our sexuality to its fullest depths (pun intended); fear of the unknown keeps us from discovering what all of our options are. Fortunately, the missionary position, although pleasant enough, is not the only thing on the menu.

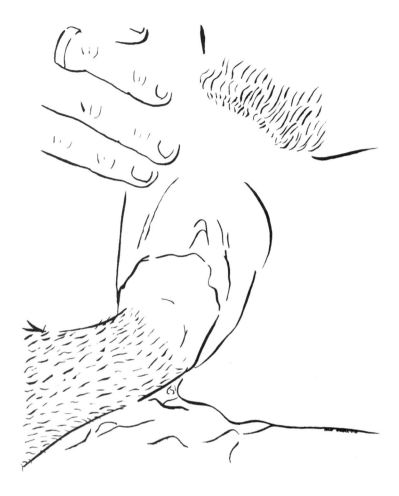

Friends and family were confused when they found out I was writing this book; they all initially assumed that by *fisting* I meant *anal* fisting. Material on anal fisting is more readily available. Even sites on the 'Net and on the Web seem to have a particularly anal focus.

Anal fisting is certainly a potent and exacting activity with many, many devotees. It is riskier than vaginal fisting and more popular among gay men – who have pioneered the dissemination of many kinds of sexual information – and thus has been better documented than its "sister" art. Now, dissemination of information is a good thing; Mama always told me that if you want to do something, you should learn how to do it right (this is especially true of anal fisting; see the reference section in back for more information). While this book won't tell you how to stuff your entire hand up someone's ass, it *will* tell you how to make the most of your manual dexterity and a cunt.

For those of you, Dear Readers, who find the word "cunt" offensive, you have my deepest apologies; no offense is intended to the vaginal community or any of its devotees. Believe me, no one has more respect for cunts than do I, being both a possessor of one and a lover of them. I specifically chose that word instead of *vagina*, *pussy*, *box*, or any number of other terms because it is short, concise, easy to say, unclinical and, in my opinion, a very friendly little word. Thanks to Dossie Easton and her groundbreaking work with the reclamation of the word "slut," I am dedicated to following in her footsteps and bringing "cunt" out of the shadows and into the light.

Our language is, at best, inadequate to the task of describing women and their sexual experiences. The words we use are either too clinical or too derogatory. Our vocabulary relegates woman to the role of passive recipient who is acted upon, instead of someone who is empowered to take the initiative and act. I have often wondered what our world would be like if the words for vagina were flattering and warm instead of crude and cold, or if the act of intercourse was called "reception" rather than "penetration," but that's another book altogether.

By adding items to the menu of our sexual practices, we can find greater pleasure and satisfaction in sexual intimacy; this book is devoted to adding vaginal fisting to that menu, from recipe to consumption. While fisting may not be everyday fare for most women – woman cannot live on fisting alone – it is likely to be an exquisite confection, a delightful addition to the menu. For those who feast on a fist at every meal, I hope this book will serve as a guide to the connoisseur, to help refine the craft and art of fisting.

So eat each other, drink each other, and be merry!

INTRODUCTION

WHAT
is this book about?

This is a book about vaginal fisting. "Fisting" may sound like a fierce and intrusive act; in truth and in appropriate practice, it is anything *but* that. For some, the word may bring to mind an image of a fist being slammed into a vagina and thrust vigorously in and out. This text is committed to the eradication of that awful, brutal image. If that's what fisting has been to you, Dear Reader, you have my profoundest sympathies. If that's what fisting has been in your experience, it has not been done correctly. Vaginal fisting – "fisting," for the sake of brevity – is the intimate, potent, sexual act of slowly, gradually inserting an entire hand into a cunt, curling it into a fist, and sending both the giver and the recipient to a fabulous place of sublime beauty and sensation.

Fisting is not something one does <u>to</u> a woman; it is something one does <u>with</u> a woman.

It is a miraculous and breathtaking thing to watch your lover's body swallow your hand, fingers at a time, until it disappears completely into her. It is a breathtaking and reverent moment when one looks down and sees one's wrist and forearm ending – or is it beginning? – in an incredible connection of flesh. When I have my lover's hand firmly encased in my cunt, I am as consumed by the passion and sexual intensity of this act as my lover's hand is consumed by my body. Time stands still for both of us; in that moment, there is only skin, only lust, only passion, only us. As a lover of mine once put it, fisting is "like being inside the heartbeat of everything."

For whom is this book written?

This book about fisting is for anyone who has a cunt or would like to get their hand(s) into one. "Fist*er*" is the term used to indicate the person who makes the fist; "fist*ee*" is the term for the person who receives the fist. While only women can be the recipients of vaginal fisting, men as well as women are able to enjoy the giving of a fist. Lesbians, bisexuals, and heterosexuals alike can enjoy the delightful experience that fisting can bring to both the fister and the fistee.

Many people that I spoke to were operating under the assumption that fisting is something you can do only if you're into S/M. Just as fisting is not exclusive to any one gender or orientation, neither is it strictly limited to the realm of sadomasochism or bondage and discipline. Fisting can definitely be an element of such experiences; in fact, it seems to be broadly associated with that dark, mysterious world of Alternative Sexual Practices. However, one certainly need not be an S/M practitioner to enjoy the powerful physical and emotional connection of fisting. This book is for those daring pioneers who brave the darkness to claim or reclaim their own sexuality and practice whichever acts appeal to them, in whatever context they choose. This book is for those who, at least occasionally, leave the lights on.

To fist, or not to fist?

Fisting is fabulous fun. I heartily recommend it. It's one of the most intimate, moving, sensual things in the universe. If you think it's something that you might like to try, read on, or maybe even read this book aloud with your partner(s), and talk about it. A lot. If it sounds like something everyone involved wants to try, talk about your ideas and desires, and go for it. Don't beat around the bush when it comes to fisting. Whether or not you're into S/M, fisting *must* be a consensual act.

If you are into S/M, and you think fisting might happen in a scene, be certain to negotiate it as a possible component *before* the scene begins. The middle of a scene is not the place to renegotiate the scene you're in the middle of. (For more information on safe, sane and consensual S/M, please see the resource guide in back).

If your partner wants to fist you but the idea puts you off, don't do it. If you want to explore being a fister and your partner says no way, back off. Pushing someone into doing something just to shut you up, or doing something someone pushes you into doing just to shut them up, is not consensual. Doing things with, to, or for someone if you are not fully willing is wrong. It's abuse.

If someone is trying to pressure you into fisting, or any other activity, you're being abused. If you can't take your lover's "no, thanks" for an answer, you may have a problem. First off, make sure that the words you use have the same meaning to the person you're using them with. Once you're assured that you both are really talking about the same thing, work on your communication skills with each other, and see if you can find a middle ground. An objective third party, such as a sex-positive therapist or counselor (see the resource guide in the back of this book for help in finding such a person), can be a huge asset to opening doors closed by a conflict about the definitions of the terms we use to discuss our thoughts and feelings.

If that gets you nowhere, and your partner is doing things to you that you don't want done, or what you're trying to do is being protested and "no" doesn't slow you down, you should immediately contact your local hotline for abusive or abused partners. Check the resource guide for contacts, or look in the front of your phone book for local resources.

As a survivor of domestic terrorism, I feel safe in saying that if your lover can't take no for an answer in the bedroom, there will be more and more other places and times when they won't feel like taking no for an answer. Never let anyone push you into any sexual activity. If the fistee is unwilling or unenthusiastic, fisting becomes a high-risk activity; tension and struggle can cause a fair amount of damage to the fragile tissue involved, and that type of damage can have serious, possibly life-threatening, ramifications.

CHAPTER ONE

A FISTING FAQ
(frequently asked questions)

Here's a list of the questions I'm most often asked, and brief answers. If you don't find the answer to your question in this section, please read on. Most of these answers are discussed in depth in other sections of the book.

Why would anyone want to do such a thing?

Because it feels lovely, awesome, beautiful, filling, satiating, breathtaking, consuming, captivating, delicious, delightful, delectable, exceptional, extraordinary, exquisite, ecstatic, divine, exciting, electrifying, excellent, intoxicating, incredible, remarkable, overwhelming, potent, mighty, powerful, hot, orgasmic, striking, rapturous, thrilling, intense, strange, wondrous, superb, splendid, marvelous, magnificent, grand, passionate, sensational, rousing, mind-boggling, inspiring, moving, poignant, stirring, exemplary, outstanding, unique, fascinating, scintillating, luscious, scrumptious, gratifying and zesty, and that's just the beginning.

Fisting offers a woman a sense of fullness that can't be had with any other item or activity. You could use a dildo the size of Detroit, and it still wouldn't fill you up the way a fist does. No offense to the penile colony, but when it comes to comparing hard-ons to whole hands, penis size really *doesn't* matter. A fist is a different shape as well as a different size, and it has more surface area and mass than a dick. Comparing a dick or dildo to a fist is like comparing hot dogs to hand grenades.

We are accustomed to experiencing sexual pleasure largely through our genitals. A cunt is a cunt twenty-four hours a day, seven days a week; it's always a genital. A dick is a dick all the time; it is always a genital. A dildo is a dildo in perpetuum; it's always a pseudo-genital. A hand is a hand all of the time; we experience a great deal of the world around us via our hands. During fisting, the hand multitasks: it's still a hand, but it becomes a genital, an additional appendage through which we can experience sexual pleasure and gratification. Moreover, it's not just the owner of the hand that gets to experience the hand as a genital; the recipient does as well. Since the hand usually isn't a genital, experiencing it as such can be pretty damn mind-blowing.

Is fisting dangerous?

If it's done correctly, no. With the right attitudes and precautions, fisting is perfectly safe. The mystique that surrounds fisting isn't because fisting is dangerous; it's because fisting isn't an everyday thing for most people, and lack of information shrouds it in a cloud of mystery.

How old should I be before I explore fisting?

There's no minimum age for being a fistee or fister. Of course, I am certain that none of you, Dear Readers, would ever engage in any sexual activity involving anyone under your local, legal age of sexual consent. As a rule, any woman who is healthy and of age is a potential fisting participant.

Do I have to have a baby before I can be fisted?

Nope. There are physiological differences between bodies that have given birth and those that haven't, but fisting isn't dependent upon those differences. Fisting may be easier for those who have given vaginal birth, but many who haven't can also enjoy it.

What does it feel like?

Fisting is an amazing, profound, and utterly delicious experience. It can make the participants feel completely connected on an intensely intimate level. It's not just a sexual experience; it involves the participants so thoroughly that it becomes a mental, emotional and even a spiritual experience. It leaves you speechless, astounded, overwhelmed, breathless, and dizzy with pleasure. It feels like no other sexual act.

As a fistee, I feel filled, fulfilled. I am swimming in a sea of pleasure; I am the tide, and my waves are lapping at the shores of my lover. I feel powerful and acquiescent. I feel wondrous.

As a fister, I feel reverent and honored by my lover's acceptance of my presence so deeply inside her. I am awed by her passion and the invitation to share it with her. I feel welcome, trusted, and entirely embraced. I feel wondrous.

Is it painful?

Evaluating whether something "hurts" is purely individual and subjective. Things that might be excruciatingly painful in a non-erotic context become intense erotic sensation between the sheets. Your endorphins, incited by desire, take your body away from places of pain. In general, there's two kinds of pain: good pain, and bad pain. Sexually, I separate them further into the categories of "hurt" and "harm." Fisting may hurt, for a moment or two, as the widest part of the hand meets the tightest part of the cunt, but after they've shaken hands and made friends, the hurt should fade into pleasurable intensity. (More about this in Chapter Five.)

When I started talking to people about fisting, those who hadn't tried it said they'd abstained largely because they thought it would hurt too much. I thought about what fisting might look like in the head of a person who'd never experienced it before. If my image of this potent and forbidden act was the brutal, forceful insertion of a fist into a cunt, then yes. I'd be put off by the fear and pain in that image; you couldn't get me to do that for all the gold under Midas's fingernails. Luckily, that's not the image I know to be true.

If you're considering fisting, try this: when you imagine it, put yourself in a warm, safe space, and in a hot, hungry frame of mind. Then let the image flow into your consciousness. Look closely at it through the eyes of your cunt or cock, and see if it perhaps takes on a whole new dimension.

Can it injure me?

Only if it's done incorrectly. For the fistee, potential fisting injuries include nicks from overly long fingernails, abrasion, bruising, and vaginal or labial tearing. All of these things are avoidable, and almost certainly won't happen to you if you follow the guidelines for safe fisting listed in this book. From a fister's point of view, a risk of injury could present itself if the fistee has really strong muscles and if the fister has wrist problems and gets overly enthusiastic. Under such conditions, spraining a wrist becomes marginally possible; people with serious tendonitis or carpal tunnel problems may not be good potential fisters.

What's involved?

Two (or more) willing participants, lots and lots of artificial lubricant, a good manicure and/or latex gloves, and communication, communication, communication. Did I mention communication? Communication is most definitely required.

Should I douche before being fisted?

No. The cunt is a self-cleaning instrument. A certain amount of discharge and distinctive scent is perfectly normal, the sign of a healthy cunt: discharge and juices are the cunt's way of flushing out unwanted organisms. One of the many symptoms of our sociocultural oppression of women is the imposition of rules about how we should smell and taste. We're taught from childhood that smelling like an earthy, sweaty animal woman is not okay; we should always smell like flowers or something equally "inoffensive." We're not even supposed to mention that women *have* a taste, let alone what flavor we should be. A woman's scent and taste may vary according to her diet and phases of the menstrual cycle; if she feels that her scent or taste is a bit on the pungent side, a warm bath or shower and a cleansing of the external genitals with gentle soap (never try to wash the inside of a cunt with soap) is usually enough to make things all nice and sniffy down there. Persistent fishy, yeasty, or otherwise unpleasant scents or a colored discharge, especially if irritation and/or itching is present, may be a sign of vaginal infection, and should be seen by a doctor.

If you douche often, and are constantly fighting symptoms like those listed above, the cause may be too much douching. When the natural balance of a cunt is disrupted by douching, good bacteria are destroyed, leaving the cunt open to infections and other problems. Douching destroys flora essential to the continued health of a cunt, and should only be done for specific, medically indicated reasons, under the direction of a knowledgeable physician.

How long will it take?

As long as it takes for you to make a short trip to heaven and back. If you are like so many of us these days and must budget out your time even more efficiently than your income, I suggest you set aside no less than two hours. If you'd like to throw in a bath in at the beginning and leave yourselves time to snuggle and come down afterwards then, to be realistic, give yourself the gift of three or four hours. It's a gift that keeps on giving.

Can you get stuck?

Nope. Not a chance. Once in a while you may feel as though you're stuck, due to a muscle spasm or vacuum lock, but if you relax, go slowly and have patience, you will once again get your hand back. (More about this later.)

I have genital piercings. Do they get in the way during fisting? Can the jewelry be dislodged?

My clitoral hood and both inner labia are pierced, and I've never had a problem with them getting in the way, nor have any of my perforated acquaintances who fist reported any difficulty. It would take a lot more that a gentle fisting to pull jewelry out of a genital piercing. If your

piercings are new, follow your piercer's instructions, and wait for at
least six weeks after your genital piercing before you give fisting a try.
Most people don't pierce their hands, but I believe that a latex glove and
a well-healed hand piercing would do just fine during a fisting
encounter.

Will it make me loose?

If a woman was fisted four or five times a day, every day, for several
years, she might begin to notice some loss of vaginal elasticity. Fisting
isn't really suited to everyday practice: not because it makes one
"loose," but because it's such a heady experience. Exercises to

strengthen your pubococcygeal muscles (see p.32) will ensure your continued tightness as well as making you a better fistee.

Can I get an STD from it?

There isn't much research being done on STD transmission rates via fisting, so empirical data is scarce. As a general rule, if you can't catch a disease from inserting a finger, you can't catch it from fisting. However, medical consensus is that fisting is of no greater risk than any other form of sexual contact where bodily fluids are involved. In fact, some sources seem to think that fisting is a low-risk activity.

If you don't have HIV or other STDs, you fist with anyone who does, and you don't use gloves of latex or another impermeable material, you're putting yourself at unnecessary risk for catching something you'd rather not have.

I have fairly large hands; how big is too big?

For the most part, size doesn't matter. I have really big hands – I can't ever buy women's gloves off the rack, and I take a large in men's gloves. I've had no difficulty fisting any of my partners. I've fisted women who haven't had kids, and women who have; I've fisted women who couldn't use even a small dildo because it was too big and hurt them. Small hands are not the key to fisting; the secrets are patience, patience, patience and lube, lube, lube, lube, lube.

If your hand is too big to fit all the way in on the first attempt, stop, and try it again some other time. Don't be disappointed; it can take several tries to make it all the way in, especially if she's young, small, and hasn't given birth or been fisted before. If, after several tries, your hand still won't fit, then your hand may be too large for that particular cunt. Some women are simply too narrow through the pelvis to take almost any fist.

Does my weight have any bearing on my becoming a fistee?

Not really, no. It's a matter of proportion; your cunt will be in proportion to your body. I am six feet tall, and weigh about one sixty-five. I probably have a larger cunt than a tiny little delicate petite woman who's five feet tall and wears a size three. As with hands, size isn't the issue; the primary factors are good muscle control, the ability to relax, the willingness to try something new, and plenty of lube.

Am I a likely fistee?

There are some health concerns that should be considered when evaluating one's fisting potential. Listed here are some physiological problems that make a woman an unlikely fistee. Fortunately, however, even if one is not suited to the position of fistee, most everyone with the patience and desire is suited to the position of fister. Fisting is a joyous experience that is just as intense from the giving end as it is from the receiving end.

Please keep in mind, as you read this section, that I must speak in general terms: there are always exceptions. The one invariable exception is a male-to-female transsexual; surgically constructed vaginas are much less elastic than the type that genetic women are born with. If you have any doubts as to your ability to become a fistee, do some research on your own so that you can have an informed dialogue, and then talk to a fisting-friendly physician. (See the resource guide in the back of this book for help in finding a physician who is knowledgeable, or at least open-minded, about fisting.)

Women who have had a history of gynecological difficulties should consult their physicians before trying to be fisted. A woman who has a history of PID (pelvic inflammatory disease) should check with her doctor. PID can cause scarring and adhesions in the abdominal area; although these are unlikely to be a problem during fisting, the stretching and pulling sensations of being fisted may be uncomfortable. If you've had PID more than once, it's important to find out why you have a recurrence of this condition. A woman with a history of sexually transmitted diseases (because of the internal scarring they can cause) should first make certain that she has nothing transmittable; then she should go slowly, ceasing her fisting activity immediately if it hurts or if she exhibits any STD symptoms.

Women who have had a muscular or skeletal injury in the pelvic area such as a broken coccyx, a hernia, or a fractured hip, and/or certain disorders such as Crohn's disease, are unlikely fistees; they should plan on revelling in the pleasure of being a fister. Endometriosis may also make being fisted uncomfortable for some women. Before you abandon all hope, check with your doctor.

I'm pregnant; must I give up fisting?

The doctors I talked to in preparing this book varied widely in their answers to this question. One felt that pregnant women should enjoy fisting only from the giving of it, stating that during pregnancy, it is unwise to stress or compress the uterus lest the fragile fetus be dislodged or damaged, or lest strong uterine contractions induce a miscarriage. Another said "Not bloody likely." And a third said "Go ahead, except between 27 and 38 weeks." Sorry I can't provide an authoritative answer here; I'd suggest that you talk this over with your own doctor and make your own decision.

Should I be fisted if I've recently had a baby, an abortion or a miscarriage?

It's medically advised that a woman who has just given birth, had a miscarriage or an abortion should wait for at least six weeks before being fisted; she should consult her physician before resuming any of her normal sexual activities. You need to give your vagina and uterus time to recover after your cervix has been dilated for childbirth or abortion.

Sometimes I have a little spotting after I've been fisted. Is that serious?

Probably not. Cunt and genital tissue is loaded with capillaries and other blood suppliers; a tiny nick or minuscule tear can happen, and then you spot. A little bit of pink on the paper right after fisting or the next day is normal, and not cause for alarm. If you notice anything unusual, such as continued pain, fever, or a copious or foul-smelling discharge, it's time to get to the doctor.

Can I be fisted during my period?

Yes, you can. But if you're the type of woman who normally loses interest in sex during your moon time, you probably won't want to be fisted. For me, however, the intense uterine contractions of a fisting orgasm help to both ease the pain of menstrual cramps, and to expedite the flow of blood leaving the uterus. It makes my period shorter and less painful (just another perk of an already fabulous activity).

If you want to be fisted during your menses, make sure you have an abundance of lube (please see the note on artificial lubricants in chapter 4). The good thing about fisting while bleeding is that the extra fluid makes for more smooth slickness. The downside is that blood is less viscous and dries much faster than cuntjuice; to avoid friction burns and sticky clumps of dried blood, use even more lube than you usually would, and add additional lube at regular intervals.

It's easy to determine your future if you're fisting a woman who's menstruating: you're sure to have your palm red (and the sheets, the towels, your clothing...).

If you're within a day or three of your period, fisting may bring it on early because of the intense uterine contractions that come with a fisting orgasm. If you're nowhere near your moontime and you begin to bleed as though you were, there may be a problem (please see the Troubleshooting appendix).

I've had an hysterectomy. Can I be fisted?

A woman who has had an hysterectomy should consult her physician; in addition to reduced levels of lubrication, there may be other factors to consider such as less (or more) space within the vaginal cavity, and reduced uterine sensation. Fisting is not impossible, but caution should be exercised while discovering her new postoperative tolerance levels.

If I'm going or have been through "The Change of Life," can I still be fisted?

Menopausal and postmenopausal women should proceed with caution; hormonal changes at that stage in a woman's life may result in a thinning of the vaginal mucosa and/or less lubrication – a condition known by the unfortunate title of "vaginal atrophy." A friend who has experienced this tells me that it feels dry, abraded, "like you had too much sex the night before, only you didn't actually enjoy the night before." A reduction in natural lubrication is easy enough to remedy with artificial lubricant, but postmenopausal women who aren't taking hormone supplements may have a thinning of the vaginal walls that dramatically increases the risk of a fisting-related tear. If you're experiencing menopausal symptoms, see your doctor about the possibility of hormone replacement therapy. If you get the go-ahead, go slow; use plenty of lube, take your time, and stop immediately if it hurts.

I'm not a spring chicken anymore. Is fisting still an option for me?

Popular sociocultural myth has it that older women have little or no sex drive; that's completely, entirely and utterly false. Age and the changes it brings to a woman's body certainly do have influence on a woman's sexuality, but those changes are not such that they render a woman dispassionately celibate. Age makes the human body more fragile; with increased fragility, a thinning of the mucosa and a reduction in lubrication, there is a slightly higher risk of injury. "Old" does not mean "withered-up and sexless." I asked one of the physicians who consulted with me on this book to estimate how old is too old to be fisted: he said, "Eighty. After that, she should check with her doctor."

CHAPTER TWO

A CUNT
owner's manual

A *user's guide*

If you have a cunt, you probably have at least a general idea about how to use it. If you are enamored of cunts, you've hopefully tried to educate yourself about the care and feeding of them. This section applies to anyone who has a cunt and wants to be able to make the most of it, and to those who wish to learn to make the most of the cunts of others. The best advice I can give to anyone who's considering learning how to use a cunt is *go slow*, and listen to what its owner tells you, both with her voice and with her body.

One basic sign of sexual arousal is a flush on the skin. Cheeks, necks, and breasts are usually the places that the skin gets flushed and warm. She'll probably start breathing more heavily, too. Do a nip check; if she has hardened, erect nipples, she's probably aroused. An increase in the amount of cuntjuice is also a sure sign of arousal. If you're not sure how to read her body, ask her where she is, and listen to what she tells you.

Self-knowledge

Trial and error is one way to learn how to do something, but not the method I'd recommend for learning fisting. It's important to know as much as possible about an engine before working on it; it's important to know something of female anatomy and genitalia before setting about to put a fist in it. There's more to a woman's nether regions than a sweet spot and a hole.

For some, this chapter will be redundant, but I chose to include this information because I have found that there are far too many women who know too little of their own bodies, and many more men who are ignorant of female anatomy. For those of you who already have a working knowledge of cunts – either your own or those of others – please consider this section a review.

To have good sex of any sort, it is imperative, essential, that both partners possess a solid sense of self-awareness, both as to their own physical construction and about what works for them. If you are uncertain about your own cunt, a hand mirror and some quiet, private time will be a tremendous help. If you are uncertain about someone else's cunt, ask her; if she is uncertain, you both can have a fine time exploring. Sexual discovery is highly erotic, whether it be done solo or in tandem. The things one learns can only serve to heighten one's sexual experiences. Spend an afternoon or evening doing some genital spelunking; it's free, it's fun, and it's delightfully informative.

Fingers are waterproof and easily cleansed; don't hesitate to employ them in your self-explorations. Feel your way around down there, teaching yourself what types of touch in which locations really work. I heartily recommend spending some extra time getting to know your clitoris intimately. Slide a finger or two into your cunt; feel the ridges, the smoothness, the silky wetness. Try sliding in another finger or two; they won't get lost. Those pleasing sensations belong to you, and you can have them whenever you like. See if you can find your "G" spot (named after some guy named Grafenberg – isn't that a hoot!). It's just inside the cunt – about an inch in on most women – and up. Put your finger in up to about the second knuckle, and make that index finger beckoning gesture (also referred to as the "come hither" motion). You'll know it when you find it (for more info, check the reference section).

For those women who ejaculate (and those who don't, please see the reference section at the back of this book), try to find the spongy tissue that holds female ejaculate. It's just inside the cunt, and up. You'll know you've found it when, with the application of a little pressure, you feel a sensation similar to yet different from the sensation that accompanies the need to urinate. Don't worry; if you empty your bladder before you begin, you probably won't pee accidentally. (I should note here that a couple of the experts I spoke to in preparing this book were extremely skeptical about the existence of the G-spot and/or the whole phenomenon of female ejaculation. While my own experience leads me to disagree strenuously, I suggest you do your own homework and decide for yourself.)

Explore. See how many fingers you can get in and around your cunt. It's fun, it feels terrific, and it will provide you with invaluable information about your body and how it works – information you can then relay to your partner(s) so that they can join you in a mutually satisfying journey to limitlessly pleasurable destinations. You may not be able to go so far as to fist yourself during this self-exploration, but I've seen pictures of it being done so I'm assured that it isn't impossible (please see Appendix II for more information on fisting yourself).

Even if you decide not to go so far as to explore your ability to fist yourself, the information you'll glean from exploring your cunt and its surroundings will be priceless in the quest to improve and expand your sexual repertoire.

Communication

Second in importance only to self-awareness and self-knowledge is being able to communicate what one knows about one's self to one's partner(s). My mother and I were having a little chat some years ago over a glass or two of wine, just after her second marriage. The subject came around to sex, as most conversations with me tend to do, and in a hushed, conspiratorial tone she confided to me that her new mate was the first man ever to give her an "organism." I laughed until I cried, and said through my tears, "Mom, if you can't talk about an orgasm, it's no wonder it took you so long to have one!"

I grew up in an environment that only allowed discussions of sex and sexuality in very clinical, physiological, mechanical terms. When I became sexually active, I was operating under the sad and erroneous assumption that there were only a very few limited forms of sexual interaction, that my partner would know all of them, and that those few, simplistic things would be completely and totally gratifying, inasmuch as women were permitted to enjoy sexual acts.

Yuk.

I have since rejected that model of sexuality and sexual interaction in favor of a sexual model that embraces self-awareness, communication, and a rewarding and hearty variety of interactions. If I don't ask for what I want, I'm not very likely to get it. Still worse: if I don't know what I want, I cannot ask for it, and I am all but assured of not getting it. Once I figured out what worked for me, I was faced with the challenge of finding a way to convey that information to my lovers.

I found that when I spoke in terms of "I" – what I liked, what I disliked, what I wanted to try, what held no interest for me – my lovers were quite receptive. They listened to what I was saying, returned the gift of information with information about themselves, and made it possible for both of us to get what worked, what we wanted. In the rare instance of a lover or potential bedmate who didn't take very well to the gift of exchanged information, I learned that those individuals were not the people who were going to help me to enlarge my sexual life and pleasure. I quickly stopped dealing with people whose ears and minds were closed, no matter how wide open their legs were spread.

Explore your body. Be creative. Learn and share what works. Fantasize. Imagine what might make your sexual life even better. One can't share information one doesn't have. The saying goes that knowledge is power; this principle is magnified when related to sexuality. The more knowledge that is shared, the more powerful sexual experiences become. Sharing knowledge about what works sexually benefits everyone involved: you get more of what you want, they get more of what they want, and everybody respects everybody else in the morning.

CHAPTER THREE

ANAT⊕MICALLY
Correct

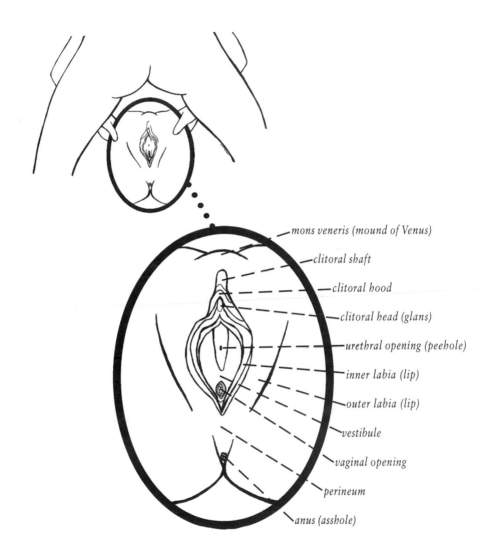

mons veneris (mound of Venus)

clitoral shaft

clitoral hood

clitoral head (glans)

urethral opening (peehole)

inner labia (lip)

outer labia (lip)

vestibule

vaginal opening

perineum

anus (asshole)

An operator's reference

The clitoris, an enormously popular little spot, is more than it appears to be. The head of the clit, usually extremely sensitive and the source of most female orgasms, is only the tip of the iceberg. The shaft, the hidden part of the clit, is buried under the folds of the clitoral hood.

During arousal, the clit fills with blood, becomes enlarged and increasingly sensitive, much like an erect penis, and retreats into the hood. If you put your fingers alongside the clit and pull the hood back a little, you'll see the beginnings of the shaft, which is connected to the muscles that attach to the membrane that defines the vaginal cavity. The labia minora, or inner lips, are attached to the clit hood and are usually quite sensitive. The labia majora, or outer lips, are the folds of skin on either side of the inner lips. On some women, they're all but invisible, seeming to be just a little extra skin between the thighs and the cunt; on some women, they're quite full and plush. They're not usually quite as sensitive as the inner lips, but they're certainly not to be neglected. Lips are, after all, for kissing.

Directly beneath the clit is the urethral opening; that's where urine and, many believe, ejaculate leave the body (for more information on the fascinating world of female ejaculation, please see the appendix in the back of this book). Fear not: the two fluids are decidedly different; one's not likely to be mistaken for the other. One smells like urine, the other one doesn't, and the tastes are very distincltly different. The urine of a healthy person is sterile, but tends to acquire bacteria on its trip past the

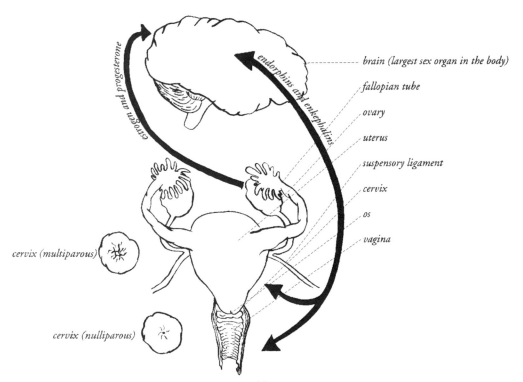

estrogen and progesterone

endorphins and enkephalins

brain (largest sex organ in the body)

fallopian tube

ovary

uterus

suspensory ligament

cervix

os

vagina

cervix (multiparous)

cervix (nulliparous)

vulva; additionally, urine can carry bugs like the HIV virus, STDs like chlamydia, and the Hepatitis B virus. Thus, if you think there might be any chance at all that you could come into contact with your partner's urine, and the two of you are not monogamous or fluid-bonded, make certain that you have a ready stock of latex or nitrile gloves and plastic wrap near at hand.

Below the urethral opening is the vaginal opening. It's surrounded by a sphincter muscle, much like the one that surrounds the anus, but it's not usually as tense as the anal sphincter. This brings us to the asshole; I'm certain that you know where yours is, and are more than likely familiar with the location of your partner's as well. But since we're not going there, let's move back up, and take a closer look at the muscles and ligaments inside a cunt.

Inside the abdominal cavity, surrounding the cunt, urethra, and rectum, is a series of muscles called the pelvic floor muscles; they're crucial for supporting the lower organs and controlling the flow of cunt traffic. The vaginal sphincter is a member of this group of muscles. It's a ring of muscle that keeps the cunt a closed, secure environment. It can be stretched to admit desirables, such as a dildo, cock, vibrator, or fist. To isolate it, put a finger or two just inside the vagina. Imagine the ring of muscle surrounding your finger as a drawstring, and pull the drawstring tight. Learning to control and strengthen this muscle will make fisting an even more enjoyable activity; having control over this muscle gives you more control over your sexual experiences, and the stronger it is, the better to hug your lover's fist with, my Dear Reader.

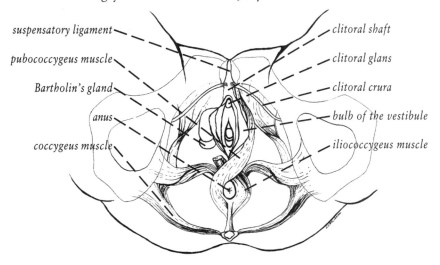

suspensatory ligament · clitoral shaft · pubococcygeus muscle · clitoral glans · Bartholin's gland · clitoral crura · anus · bulb of the vestibule · coccygeus muscle · iliococcygeus muscle

Vaginismus is a reflexive tensing of the vaginal sphincter and other pelvic floor muscles that makes penetration painful and difficult if not impossible. It often but not always takes place in women who've had traumatic experiences with penetration. If that's what happens to you at the thought of having anyone put anything in your cunt – let alone an entire fist – it's not all in your head. Your reaction to penetration anxiety is valid, and vaginismus is usually treatable.

The most significant of the pelvic floor muscles to fisting, next to the vaginal sphincter, is the pubococcygeal or PC muscle. It may not be politically correct, but it's definitely anatomically correct. Isolating the PC muscle is important because it's one of the major muscles that you'll need to be able to relax enough to admit a fist.

To isolate it, put a finger in your cunt and give that finger a hug. If that isolation technique doesn't work for you, try stopping the flow of urine the next time you go. Be sure your legs are apart when you try, or you may confuse the urinary sphincters with the PC muscle. The PC muscle is easy to train; after you've isolated it, flex, hold for two or three seconds, and release – an exercise called Kegel exercises. Repeat often. It's not like anyone can tell that you're working out, and you don't need a membership to a gym to do the exercise. By strengthening this muscle, you'll have better control over it, including the relaxing of it. The more relaxed you can make this muscle, the more easily you'll be able to accommodate a fist.

Once a fist has made it past the vaginal sphincter, most of what surrounds it are the vaginal walls. These walls are very elastic, and vary in texture between almost smooth to quite ridged; the more distended they become in their efforts to accommodate a fist, the smoother they will become. Compared to the tissue that lines the rectum, the vaginal walls are loaded with nerve endings. The farther up in the vaginal cavity, the fewer the nerve endings specific to pleasure – but, during arousal, the uterus and cervix lift up out of the way, and the vaginal canal expands to two or three times its normal size and becomes extremely sensitive to pressure. This heightened sensitivity, both to pleasure and pressure, is one of the things that makes vaginal fisting less of a risky proposition than anal fisting; if an abrasion or nick occurs, it's more likely to be felt, and can be dealt with promptly and appropriately.

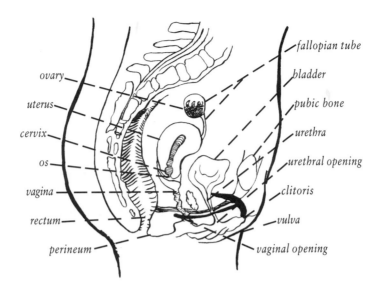

ovary

uterus

cervix

os

vagina

rectum

perineum

fallopian tube

bladder

pubic bone

urethra

urethral opening

clitoris

vulva

vaginal opening

At the far end of the vagina lies the cervix. Inside a woman's body, the uterus resembles an upside-down pear; the cervix is the only part of the uterus that protrudes into the vagina. If you reach in and touch it, you'll find that it feels very much like a nose. The rest of the uterus is suspended in the abdominal cavity, above the suspensory ligaments that can be felt to either side of the cervix.

On the bottom of the cervix is the os, the opening into the uterus through which semen passes on its way into the uterus and a fetus passes on its way out. The os will feel like a slight indentation in the cervix. The opening itself is usually too small to feel, but it is larger in women who have given birth (multiparous) than in women who haven't (nulliparous).

Don't try to put anything in the cervix through the os; it's a very bad idea. The uterus has very specific reasons for existing; being a container for foreign objects is not one of its intended uses. The uterus is a sterile area. If you try to put anything foreign in it, you're breaking the seal, and opening yourself up to a world of bacteria and viruses, and you're just begging for a nasty case of PID or endometritis. Trying to insert anything into the uterus is a great way to end up with, at best, a nasty infection and, at worst, permanent scarring that can really mess up lots of essential female bodily functions, including menstruation, conception and gestation.

Additionally, the inside of the uterus lacks the pleasure receptors and nerve endings that result in pleasurable sensations; playing with it won't make you swoon with delight, and it could result in some very icky conditions. Play where it feels good, and leave the working parts alone to do their jobs.

A manual manual

Cunts are very important to fisting. Without them, fists would have to stick to pockets and brawls. Fists are just as important to fisting; so much so, in fact, that the experience was named after them. Without fists, cunts would be limited to digits and dildos and penii (Oh my!). When we put the two together – cunts and hands – we get the potential to have orgasms hand over fist.

Cunts are very sensitive. If you have a jagged fingernail or even a hangnail, the cunt your hand is communing with will know it right away. Before you start slipping your fingers in her cunt, have a manicure. Many salons offer this service for men as well as women. If you don't want to lay out the cash or explain to your manicurist why you want such short nails and no polish, thank you, then give yourself one. You may be thinking, "Why should I get a manicure (or give myself

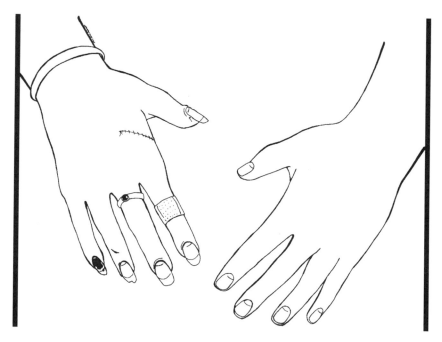

one) if I'm just going to put on a glove?" Rough nails can puncture a glove, letting bugs in; if a claw can poke through a glove, it can poke into a cunt. Any rupture in your barrier can put both of you at risk, so even if you're going to wear a glove, have a care to your fingers and her cunt.

File the nails down as short as you can get them (a metal nail file will work, but emery boards are inexpensive, come in a variety of grits and you can usually file nails more precisely and smoothly with an emery board than a file – although the deluxe files which use diamond or sapphire dust as an abrasive have a dedicated cult following). A good rule of finger is that if you have enough nail to scratch your nose, you have enough nail to scratch her cunt. Vaginal tissue is fairly tough with a goodly amount of elasticity, but it is more than fragile enough to be vulnerable to the gouge of a fingernail. A nick or tear in the cunt can open the door to many microscopic, opportunistic germs and bacteria (which human hands are loaded with – especially under fingernails, even if you wash meticulously). Don't file your nails down to the quick, but do grind them to a halt.

You'll also want to snip any stray hangnails with a pair of clippers or cuticle scissors. Don't snip them so far down that you draw blood. If you put an ungloved, bleeding finger in a cunt, both of you are at much greater risk for disease transmission. Even if you're monogamous and fluid bonded and have decided not to use gloves while fisting, you don't want to have a raw cuticle in a cunt because it can hurt. Some women are more acidic than others, and cuntjuice in a raw hangnail can sting mighty unpleasantly. To do a hangnail check, pour some isopropyl rubbing alcohol or vinegar on your hands (be sure to rinse it off thoroughly before you fist anyone). If you have any hangnails or raw cuticles, you'll feel a noticeable stinging. Pay special attention to those areas.

Avoid nail polish, even if it's just a clear sealer or topcoat. It can cause an allergic reaction vaginally, and it could chip, leaving a foreign body in the cunt that could trigger an infection. Polish that peels or lifts creates a very sharp edge that could abrade the vaginal walls and provide an opening for bacteria.

Palms aren't the only part of a hand that can reveal information. Interpersonal relations studies have shown that women have a tendency to respond better to men who take care of their hands; it's seen as a reflection of good personal hygiene habits and a sensitive eye for detail. Hands speak volumes about the people they're attached to. Lesbians, when evaluating new acquaintances, often look for the "Dutch Boy" manicure (so called because of the dyke in which the Dutch boy of fable had his finger. It's a very believable myth; I know I'd willingly put at least one finger in a wet dyke, even if my hometown *wasn't* at stake!) – it's two or more very short nails, usually on the dominant hand.

If you can't bear to sacrifice that Dragon Lady manicure or those nails that you've been growing out forever for the sake of sexual ecstasy, don't panic. You won't need to forego fisting just because you have nails and can't stand the thought of parting with them. You *will* need to wear a glove, even if you are fluid bonded, though. Stuff the tips of your glove with cotton balls – one or two in each fingertip is sufficient. Or, better yet, tape the cotton balls around and under your fingernails, then wear double gloves. Use more cotton balls if you need to in order to make certain that your nails won't work through the cotton and the glove. I suggest doing this ahead of time, when you're laying out all the other supplies. You might want to prepare two or three gloves because of Murphy's Law, or just in case. It's better to have them and not need them than it is to need them and not have them. Besides, you can always save them for next time.

CHAPTER FOUR # FISTING & SAFETY
Like hand in glove

A note on artificial lubricants

Artificial lubricants are getting their own special section because lube is absolutely essential to fisting. Many lubricants contain ingredients that have been shown to be effective in killing STD bugs and the AIDS virus, and so they become a part of safer-sex practice, as well a crucial element of positive fisting experiences.

Artificial lubricants are exactly that: artificial. No lube that I've tried has ever been exactly like cuntjuice (if somebody were to make one, I'd buy stock in the company and purchase the stuff by the gallon). When I talk about lube, I'm talking about the bottle of slippery, slidey, slick wet stuff that you bought at your local sexuality shop or ordered from a catalog; I'm not talking about all that yummy, hot, tasty, anima-scented girljuice that comes out of an aroused cunt. No matter how juicy a cunt you're dealing with, when it comes to fisting, there's no such thing as too much lube. There's lots of factors that can reduce the amount of natural lubrication a cunt produces:

* any sort of medication or drug that causes cottonmouth (from antihistamines to narcotics and marijuana, plus antidepressants, alcohol and speed);

* pre-, post-, and menopausal hormone changes;

* different phases in the menstrual cycle;

* disturbed sleep patterns, anxiety, depression and other life stresses;

* nervousness or self-consciousness with a new sex partner, or fear regarding the upcoming event.

This isn't a comprehensive list, by any means. If you've noticed a change in the amount of juice you produce, take a look at things or changes that are going on in your life; it may be that a simple, overlooked factor is causing the change. If you're concerned about a difference in your juice production and can't isolate a probable cause, talk to your doctor.

Even if everything in your life is fine, and you make plenty of juice, it still isn't enough for fisting. Luckily, a wide range of artificial lubricants are on the market (please see the reference section for lube source suggestions if you don't have a sexuality shop in your area).

Before you choose your lube, there are some factors to be considered. Lubricants that have spermicidal or antiviral agents (such as nonoxynol-9) often have an aftertaste that will range from mildly annoying to unbearably icky. If you want the safest sex possible, you want to be sure your lube has bug-killers in it. If you're having the safest sex possible, you won't be able to taste the lube. If you plan to have safe sex but think you might come into oral contact with the lube, consider the aftertaste. To avoid the taste, you can do oral things first and then add the lube later (the obvious problem with this is that you might decide you want to lick her while fisting), or you can place plastic wrap or a dental dam over the lower half of your face, or you can add flavored water-soluble gels to the lube to try and mask the taste.

Another downside to lubes with bug-zappers in them is that many women develop a sensitivity to agents like nonoxynol-9. Reactions to these agents can range from mild irritation and/or itching to blisters (vaginal and labial) and severe pain. If you're trying a new lube, do a patch-test. Place a small amount of the lube on one of your outer lips. Do something quiet for fifteen minutes or so, so that you can focus on your body's response to the lube. If nothing happens, it should be safe to use (but remember that intolerances to chemical agents can be built up over time – what works tonight may give you a rash next month – just listen to what your body has to say about it). If you have a reaction to the lube, try a different brand; that one isn't the goo for you. Some people who can't tolerate nonoxynol-9 do well with an alternative called octoxynol-8, which is available in a lube called *Gynol 1* and a few others.

When using latex barriers, such as gloves, dental dams and condoms, *never* use an oil-based lubricant such as vaseline, vegetable oil, massage oil or hand lotion. Oils eat latex. If the structural integrity of your barrier is compromised, so is your health. I also discourage the use of oil-based lubes for fisting because they have a tendency to not clean up well, and the residue they can leave in the vaginal cavity is fine fodder for infection.

There's no need to resort to oil-based lubes for fisting fun; there's scads of water-based lubes available (with and without bug-zappers). Choosing a lube is a very personal thing; find the one you like best. Many companies make sample packets; pick some up at your local erotic boutique or mail-order emporium and experiment. I favor a brand called *Wet Light* (it also comes in a regular version that has nonoxynol-9 in it and the company that makes it is quite socially conscious). Other good brands include (but certainly aren't limited to!) *AstroGlide, Probe, Probe Light, Slippery Stuff* and *Liquid Silk*. Whichever lube works best for you is the right lube for you to use. When making your selection, read the label; lubes with glycerin or sugars in them tend to get sticky, and may cause yeast infections in women who are sensitive to them. I recommend keeping a cup of water handy, too; if your lube gets thick or "tacky," you can stretch out your supply by adding a few drops of water instead of applying more lube. Whichever way you go, keep in mind that one simply cannot have an overabundance of lubrication when placing a fist within the powerful and delicate confines of a cunt.

What is "safe" sex?

There's no such thing as "safe" sex anymore. If you enjoy munching down on a hot box lunch at the "Y," there's no such thing as a "free" lunch. But there are things you can do to help keep the tab to a minimum.

You're considering a fluid bonded relationship, in which the two of you agree to have only safer sex with your other partners (if any). You *and* your partner have had an HIV/STD test three months after your most recent possible risk of exposure (and additional HIV tests at six and twelve months, just to be sure). Neither one of you has unprotected sex with anyone else during this time, and both of you have been practicing safer sex with each other. You get the results from the last HIV tests, and on your twelve-month testaversary, you celebrate by becoming "fluid-bonded." You've both been eagerly anticipating this moment, and the sexual energy between you is off the scale; you may even have planned a ritual around burning the condom or dental dam box (don't burn the latex; it smells really nasty). Given these precautions, and assuming your continued adherence to the agreements you've made, the odds are that you're both totally clean and won't give each other anything but a really good time and some fabulously intense orgasms.

Safer sex: tools of the trade-off

You're with a new partner, or you have no intention of being monogamous (for some ideas about healthy non-monogamy, see the resource list), and you've decided that celibacy isn't for you. Safer sex lets you have your fur pie and eat it, too. There's a lot of equipment available for safer sex practice. Some of these tools are pretty amusing to look at (it took a partner and me half an hour to figure out how a dental dam harness worked – there weren't any instructions!), and a good laugh always helps to lighten the mood and enhance intimacy. Most of the stuff out there isn't terribly erotic, but my partner is (especially when she's all naked and writhing and yummy-looking), and I know that I am most certainly an erotic being, so we can usually find a way around the minor encumbrance of safer sex paraphernalia. I'd rather spend a minute or two fussing with and cussing at the dental dam harness than forego the precautions and acquire a bug that might put a real crimp in my agenda.

Try to see it this way: instead of complaining about needing to use barriers in order to have sex, consider that without the barriers, you'd either be forced to give up sex entirely (perish the thought!), or be forced to accept the unwelcome addition of a fatal virus to the family of cells that is your body. Hmmmmm... celibacy and/or death, versus barriers... celibacy... barriers... death... barriers... I don't know about you, but I definitely find myself on the barrier side of that little internal debate. In fact, when snuggled in my lover's arms, afterglowing, with a mind numbed by orgasmic delight, I actually get grateful that the barriers – damn things – are available!

I remember hearing this when I was a child: "Don't put that in your mouth! You don't know where it's been!" Human hands go to a great many places during the course of a day, and we don't usually give much thought to our daily manual adventures. Before a fisting encounter, be sure to wash both hands and a goodly portion of your forearms with a gentle antibacterial soap. Rinse off very well; remember that soaps often leave a residue on the skin, and vaginal tissue is very sensitive to possible irritants (like soap residue). People with dry skin often put

lotion on after washing their hands, but lotions can have the same effect as soap residue and other chemicals (for more useful information on the subject of hands and chemicals, please read MJ Matson's story in the back of this book). It's her "mouth" that your putting your hand into; it's your job to make sure that you know where it's been, and take appropriate measures.

Boy Scouts are always prepared; I'm not sure if Girl Scouts get the same training, but it's never too late to start your own Fisting Preparedness Plan. On your nightstand, in your toy bag or in some other handy location, you'll have a ready supply of the following items:

* a box of latex examination gloves, in a size that's snug enough for you to feel what you're doing but not so tight that they might tear (two boxes if you and your partner's hands are not in the same size range). If you or your partner is allergic to latex – an increasingly common phenomenon – fear not: nitrile and vinyl gloves are also available. Most gloves come in powdered and non-powdered versions; the powder is designed to make it easier to get your hand into and out of them. I prefer gloves that aren't powdered; I usually don't have any trouble getting them on or off, and I don't get those annoying little powder pellets when my hand inevitably begins to sweat. (Additionally, a growing number of people are allergic to talc.) If I decide I want a little powder in my lovemitt, it's easier to put some baby powder or cornstarch in a non-powdered glove than it is to try and get the powder out of a pre-powdered glove.

  "Opera-length" gloves are also available (a fancy one from a leather store is pictured on the cover of this book); you can buy them through a veterinary supply catalog or store, or at a well-equipped leather store or erotic boutique. They cover the hand, wrist, and forearm up to the elbow. They're a bit more expensive and a tad more difficult to come by, but if you wish to assure yourself of total barrier coverage, then they're the way to go.

* a jumbo, economy-sized container of artificial lubricant.

* a cup of water, perhaps in a pump or spray bottle for one-handed operation.

* some towels or "chux" (they're absorbent on one side and moisture-proof on the other, single-use, disposable, available at large drugstores and medical supplys tores, and not terribly expensive).

* if you're not in bed, grab something – a sheet or blanket – to throw over furniture to protect it from lube, juice, and ejaculate.

CHAPTER FIVE

FISTING
the adventure

You've taken off *all* of your jewelry (except any permanent or brand-new body piercing jewelry), including bracelets and watches. You've done some exploring. You've opened up communications with your partner(s). You've got your safer-sex supplies within reach of your nicely manicured hands. You and a lover or two are ready to roll in the hay.

A very good rule of thumb concerning any physical activity, especially an activity that's new to you or a lover, is "if it hurts, don't do it." In the case of fisting, that's not entirely true. Odds are that some of the very intense sensations involved in fisting may border on or become discomfort, at least the first time. By first time I mean first attempt; it may very well take more than one attempt before enough relaxation and stretching is done to accommodate a fist, and some women simply are not physically constructed to be fistees. Neither the fistee nor the fister should despair if the first attempt does not result in a complete fisting. As long as you've had a good time, you've done a successful fisting.

If the attempt is made correctly, though, the fistee most likely won't mind a great deal if it hurts just a little. If the fister is conscientious and pays attention to the fistee's verbal and nonverbal (body language can speak volumes) feedback, no physical or emotional damage should be done. However, if it hurts either one of a you *a lot*, it's time to back off and rethink things. The vaginal musculature, the membranes that attach the uterus to the vaginal cavity, and the uterus itself are all intended to be flexible.

Always remember to listen to your body – or your lover's, as the case may be – and stop if, at any time, the sensations move away from intensity and towards pain. If pain becomes the overriding sensation and does not readily and quickly subside, *immediately* stop what you're doing and communicate about the sensations you're both experiencing. You may need simply to slow down, or you may need to move on to something else and try fisting again at some future time. Pain is the body's response to potentially harmful stimuli; it's our alarm system. It's the body's way of telling us that all is not right; something needs to change or stop. When the body starts talking pain, *listen*.

Creating sacred space

Whenever a cunt is present, so is sacred space – a place of spiritual communion, of connection with pleasure and creation. An environment in which fisting is going to happen should be as welcoming and pleasant as a cunt. Set up all the stuff you might need ahead of time; having to futz with supplies in the middle of things is a real mood-breaker.

Take your time. Do whatever it is that relaxes you the most. Avoid using artificial relaxants, such as alcohol, pot, or other drugs. Amyl or butyl nitrate (commonly known as "poppers") have a reputation for lightening the mind and relaxing muscles, but they're dangerous and often illegal (for more information on how drugs can make fisting a scary and fatal activity, please see appendix III).

Here are some of my personal rituals that help me get into a fisting space:

I'm fortunate enough to live near the ocean; a nice long walk on the beach, arm-in-arm with my lover, is a sensual experience that really keys me in to her body and presence. The waves that caress the beach and the sound of the pounding surf are similar to the pounding insistence of my inner tides when I'm aroused. I always feel deeply in touch with my body after a beach walk, and from that space I can easily reach out and wash over my lover. If you aren't close to the beach, try a walk on the shores of a lake, or along the bank of a river or stream. There's something magical about running water.

If you're thoroughly landlocked, there's always the tub. A nice, hot bath with scented mineral salts is lovely. I avoid bubble bath before sex; it can irritate my cunt. I prefer my lover to avoid it also, because I don't like eating a cunt that tastes like soap. It's too reminiscent of having my mouth washed out as a child – a very negative association. I enjoy having my lover in the tub with me; it's a gentle sensuous experience, and it assures us both of good personal hygiene. Some body scents are quite pleasant; I'm fond of Woman Aroused and Clean Cunt, but I don't much care for Eau de Hard Day at Work. A hot bath leaves the skin warm, soft and supple and, as we all know, a woman cleansed is a delight to caress. Hot baths and caressing clean women are relaxing, and when I'm relaxed, I'm more receptive to my lover's attentions.

When I'm relaxed, my eyes become very light-sensitive. Anything over sixty watts will give me a migraine. Groping in the dark is not the answer to my dilemma; I prefer to see my lover's body, to fondle and caress her with my eyes. I want to have enough light to see what I'm doing and where I put the lube, but not so much light that I'm blinded or have to say, "Not tonight, Dear – I have a headache." Candles are my compromise. I look better by the forgiving illumination of candlelight, and the soft, warm glow of candles is romantic. If you use candles, make sure to have one large enough to last as long as you need it to, and place them someplace where they're unlikely to start a fire should you become distracted. For those who are disturbed by the flickering of candles, dimmer switches for your lamps are cheap and easy to install.

Foreplay

The importance of foreplay both to a woman's overall sexual experience and specifically as an adjunct to fisting cannot be overestimated. Along with getting the libido and the mind into the same space, there are essential physiological changes that occur during arousal that can make or break a fisting encounter. When a woman is aroused, when she is able to turn off the left-brain thinking processes and she *becomes* her body, she becomes enthusiastically responsive to things that would, outside of an aroused setting, not be possible. Fisting is one of those things.

"Foreplay" is a very general term which encompasses any and all activities that feel good to the participants, and which lead to higher states of arousal. Thirty minutes of sweet, soft kisses and tender, loving caresses qualifies as foreplay; thirty minutes of begging for sex does not. What qualifies as foreplay to one woman might be anathema to the next. If there's any doubt as to what turns her on, ask. If she's not sure, try this: get cozy with her and this book in a comfortable place. Go back to the Cunt Owner's Manual, and take turns reading it aloud to each other. Then put what you've read into action. For me, just wrapping my lips and tongue around the words we use to talk about sex is an erotic activity. Talking about sex is sometimes more intimate than doing it, because you must truly invest yourself in the exchange. Sex involves the body; talking about sex involves the mind as well.

It may take several attempts before she's ready to receive an entire fist. That's not unusual, especially for younger women and women who have not given vaginal birth. It may be that she must work up to engulfing a fist; the catch is that all of the working up to a fist must happen while she's all worked up. Even if it does take more than one attempt, it will not be possible at all for her to receive an entire fist if the attempts are not made while she is aroused.

Foreplay not only begins the process of encouraging the mind to let go so that the body can take over; it also has some very physical results. The cunt begins to get all nice and juicy, and the inner two-thirds eventually doubles in diameter. The uterus lifts up into the pelvic cavity, moving itself out of the way to leave more room inside the cunt. Increased blood flow to the breasts and genitals heightens their sensitivity; the nipples become erect, the inner lips swell and deepen in color. Endorphin levels rise. The heart rate increases; pulses pound, and breathing becomes faster and heavier, circulating more oxygen into the blood, which helps the muscles. The muscles involved, from the vaginal sphincter to the PC muscle to the pelvic floor, begin to relax; with these muscles relaxed, her body is more likely to be able to receive a fist.

When a woman is aroused, things that normally feel good feel even better, and things that weren't possible become possible. Watching a woman rise to meet herself and her desires as she becomes aroused is an incredibly hot experience; take the time to enjoy it not just as a means to an end, but in and of itself. It's a powerful feeling, coming into your body fully like that, and it's incredibly stimulating to watch her as she rises. The hotter she gets, the more likely she'll be able to swallow a fist.

Getting your fingers wet

Once you've both gotten really hot from plenty of yummy foreplay, and have gotten into a position comfortable for both of you, you're ready to embark on this fantastic journey. Don't try this if you have an appointment with the dentist or your accountant in an hour; fisting is something that should never be rushed. If either one of you is distracted or in a hurry, the risk of injury increases dramatically. If you're in the mood for a quickie, fisting isn't likely to meet your needs. Have lunch on your lunch hour; fisting is more like a five-course meal with wine and dessert, and maybe even some fine Port and an after-diner cigar, that

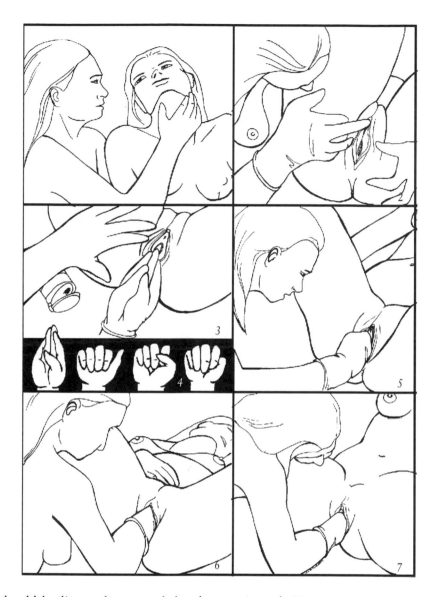

should be lingered over and deeply experienced. Fisting in general – especially the first encounter – may take a considerable amount of time and patience. Make sure you have plenty of time and privacy.

Establish a warm, intimate link. Make contact with each other through lots of eye contact, kissing, touching, stroking, tickling, sucking, licking, and whatever works for you. It's important to get close; fisting is an act of trust, and trust is much easier to do if everyone's on the same page. I recommend cunnilingus as part of the connecting process; not only does it warm you up and get the juices flowing, but it gives you a chance to get down there and have a look around.

Glove up. It's a good idea to glove both hands, as you'll be frequently reapplying lube with your free hand. It's tough to tell cuntjuice and lube apart by looking, and a fluid exchange you aren't aware of can harm you. Lube your hand and her cunt generously (remember to heat the lube in a bowl of warm water beforehand – a cold slimy jolt of goo between her legs is not the best way to get started). Go slow. Start with one or two fingers; wait for her to give you either a nonverbal or verbal signal that her body is ready for more. As she becomes more and more aroused, her cunt will start to open up, and there will be more space to add additional fingers (one at a time, unless she asks for more). She may even say something like "I'm hungry... I want more of your hand inside me... now."

Add some more lube. A good rule of thumb (and index and pinky, too) is to add lube each time you add a finger. Slide in a third finger, and then a fourth. Ask her how she's doing. Save the thumb for last. Masturbating with a vibrator or being eaten during the insertion process works best for me; it helps me relax the muscles, and raises my level of arousal. Other women prefer not to have their clit stimulated so that

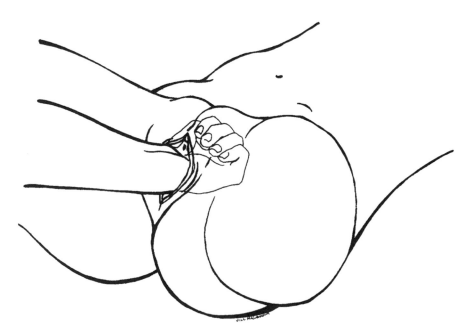

they can concentrate on the building tension, anticipating what's going to come next.

When you've worked up to all four fingers and the thumb, make a "duck"; it's the same finger configuration as the one you'd use to hold in front of a light to make a cute, quacky shadow on the wall. (Look at the first hand shown in the series of four hands in the illustration on the previous page to see what I mean.) Let her know how many fingers you have in; tell her how beautiful she is, how great she's doing, and how incredibly hot her cunt sensuously and completely wrapping itself around your hand is making you. I find, more often than not, that my hand naturally goes in palm up, so that I'm looking down at the inside of my wrist. If she's on her hands and knees in a rear-entry position, I'm looking at the back of my hand and wrist. Rather than trying to remember which side of my wrist is supposed to be part of the scenery of a certain position, I remind myself that my palm should be facing her belly, not her spine. When I'm all the way in, it's easier to curl my fingers into a fist if my hand is palm-up (if she's on her back); I don't feel like I need to worry as much about gouging her cunt as I curl my fingers.

When you've slowly and gently worked all of your fingers in, and you're in up to the bridge – the widest part of the hand – let her know. Check in with her to see how she's handling your fingers. Tell her she's almost there; gently remind her to breathe, and relax the vaginal sphincter and PC muscles. Put more lube on your hand and her cunt (moments like this make flip-top lids or pumps on your lube bottle extra special). When you have a big, slippery, gooey mess, and you're sure you've used more than enough lube, add some more. It's rather easy to underlube your hand, but it's almost impossible to overlube it. (I have heard that some women find that too much lube makes it difficult for them to come. If this is your experience, tell your partner so. Unless you have information to the contrary, though, I'd use a whole lotta lube.)

If it still feels pretty tight, or as if the bridge might not go through the vaginal sphincter, gently open and close your fingers. It's the same motion you'd make if you were making a hand puppet talk, and it looks like a squid does when it uses its arms for sucking in food. That should give you the little bit of additional stretch to help get your bridge through her tunnel.

When you're both ready, ease the bridge through, and marvel as your entire hand is consumed by her cunt. Watch her while you're doing it; she'll most likely have an astounding look on her face, and it's thrilling to watch her cunt envelop your whole hand.

Occasionally, fisting can just "happen." One of my early fisting experiences was something of a surprise. It was one of those times when every intimate, sexual detail was clicking naturally into place. Both of us were even more hot and hungry than usual. I kept demanding more and more of her hand, and we found that somehow, all of a sudden, her entire hand had been swallowed up by my steaming, greedy cunt. It was remarkable; I don't recall feeling even so much as a twinge when the bridge of her hand went through the ring of vaginal sphincter muscle. It's not happened that way very often since, but when it does, it's due to lots and lots of foreplay, and even more lube.

Because of the space constraints inside her, it will happen naturally that your hand will curl into a ball. There just isn't enough room in there for your fingers to stay rigid. Tuck your thumb under the other four fingers, so that the surface of your fist is a smooth as possible. (See the fourth hand in the series of four in the illustration.) If you leave your thumb on top of your fingers, that digital protrusion is likely to poke her and cause discomfort.

Once you're in, pause. Savor the moment. Revel in the intensity. Appreciate the overwhelming sense of awe and being honored by this amazing reception. Take a moment to let her get used to your hand. Observe how your hand suddenly ends abruptly where she begins. Congratulations; you're officially a fister!

If your lover has made it to the rank of fister with you, then you have achieved the rank of fistee. I'd congratulate you, but you're probably feeling too good to notice. Gently press down on your abdomen; you'll be able to feel your lover's fist resting inside of you. If you can, curl up a little (or use a mirror) and look at your cunt. Notice how amazing it is to have someone so completely connected to you, who begins where you end. Grasp your lover's free hand, and lay it palm-down on your belly. Place your hand over your lover's, and push down a little. Watch your lover's eyes get even wider than they already are. Feel her pulse as the blood courses through the engorged vaginal tissue; it will feel like you have your hand wrapped around her beating heart. Feel your heartbeat as it pulses around the presence of your lover's fist; you may even notice the astounding phenomenon of your hearts beating in synch with each other. Don't be surprised, when your lover looks up at you, to see the crystalline twinkle of a tear forming in the corner of an eye. Don't be surprised if the mate to that tear appears on your own cheek.

It's time to think about moving. Add some more lube. When you're both ready, start to gently rock your fist forward and back in her cunt. Keep your motions slow and understated until she asks for more; keep in mind that all those lovely nerve endings in her cunt are being stimulated in a very intense way, and that every move you make is going to be magnified. Experiment with different types of motion. Try gently clenching and unclenching your fist, like a beating heart. You probably won't be able to open your hand up all the way, but you won't need to for her to feel it. You can gently rotate your fist back and forth. You can add an in-and-out rocking motion to the twisting: it's similar to the motion you use with a screwdriver. If I'm being fisted by a lover with smallish hands, and I'm quite aroused, my lover can pull her fist almost all the way out and then slide it back in again. If it's your first time, or she has a small cunt and you have big hands, you might not want to try that technique right off the bat. Go slow. Add lube often. Ask what feels best. Be sure to tell your fister what works and what doesn't. Your own rhythm will emerge; you'll find yourselves dancing to it without thinking about it.

Fisting orgasms are the most intense orgasms I've ever experienced, both as a fister and a fistee. If you've ever wondered what a woman's orgasm feels like from her perspective, fisting is a great way to find out. You'll feel her orgasm as it starts to build; the ripples and contractions of her muscles will talk to you. When she comes, her uterus will push down on your fist, and the vaginal walls will squeeze your hand with an impressive amount of pressure. It's unlikely that her orgasm will force your hand out of her cunt, but if it does, don't worry. If she doesn't force your fist out of her cunt, it's entirely possible that the pressure bearing down on a fist that's been clenched for a period of time may cause a hand cramp. If you hand does begin to cramp when she orgasms, I'm afraid you'll just need to ride it out for a few seconds. When she's done, and she wants you to, gently extract your fist, stretch your fingers, and rub your hand. No matter how bad the cramping may be, *never* yank your hand out suddenly. Tense vaginal muscles may tear if you attempt a too-sudden extraction. The cramps will pass.

At the same time the pelvic floor muscles are contracting around your fist, the vaginal sphincter is contracting also, firmly encasing your wrist. Experiencing my lover's orgasm in such an immediate, consuming way is one of the hottest experiences I've ever had. The mind-melting experience of watching her cum and feeling her orgasm from the inside is enough to make me have one right along with her. When I'm being fisted, I am acutely aware of my body, and of the compelling presence of my lover within me. I'm both vaginally and clitorally orgasmic; my favorite thing to do is use a vibrator to masturbate myself to orgasm clitorally while my lover gently pounds her fist into me. When I orgasm in both places at the same time, I feel as though my head is exploding. That kind of orgasm is the only kind that's ever (literally) knocked me unconscious.

Extraction

After the storm has passed, it's time to extract your fist from her cunt. Don't be alarmed if you start to pull back and find that your fist doesn't seem to want to leave its nice, cozy nest. If that happens, don't try to yank your fist out by pulling harder. Try to hold as still as you can; without the help of her now-spent passion, she's going to feel every little move you make even more intently. The contractions that accompany a woman's orgasm are so powerful that her muscles may have created a vacuum around your fist.

To gently break the seal, moisten a finger of your free hand (lube the glove on your free hand or use a lubricated finger cot), and slowly, gently slide it along your wrist or the back of your hand into her cunt. (Note: this illustration shows an extraction in which the finger is run along the palm of the hand, but depending on the position you're in and the individual anatomy of the fistee, the back or side of the hand may work better. Experiment.)

You won't need to go in very far; you'll know you've broken the seal when you feel the squeeze loosen up a bit. As you begin to slide your fist out of her cunt, uncurl your fingers; the unfurling of your fingers will occur naturally. It's not possible to pull your hand out of her while it's still balled up in a fist. Go slow, slower, slowest. Ask her if she wants you to pull out faster; if she does, she can help you by pushing down on your hand. Now you have both hands free to pet and snuggle, basking in the afterglow.

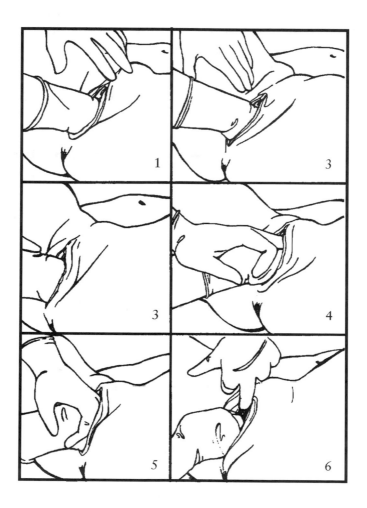

Positions

As with all works of art, each woman is uniquely different; no two are built exactly the same way. Because a fist occupies the vaginal cavity so completely, it may take some experimenting to find the position that's most comfortable for the participants. The best positions for fisting are those that cause the least amount of strain for the fister as well as the fistee. You can get leg cramps from being in an awkward position for too long. A fister can get a hand or wrist cramp from an awkward position combined with restricted, repetitive motion. Distractions like that almost invariably happen when you're just a few short strokes away from bliss; interruptions like that are frustrating. It's best to plan ahead, and find positions that reduce the chance of those annoying little physical intrusions. Here are some suggestions; they aren't written in stone. Please use them as springboards, and adapt them to suit your needs and desires. You're only limited by your limberness and imagination.

Some women find it most comfortable to be fisted in a recumbent position with their legs elevated on pillows;

that's a fairly easy position to stay in for long periods of time. Others prefer entry from behind, as with the "doggie-style" position.

Scoot to the edge of the bed, and you have available a couple of variations. Kneel with your knees towards the edge of the bed, putting your arms behind you for support. Arch back a little; this provides excellent access for the fister. This position can be difficult to maintain for long periods of time so unless you're in really good shape or you know that you can work up to fisting fairly quickly, this probably isn't the position for you to start with.

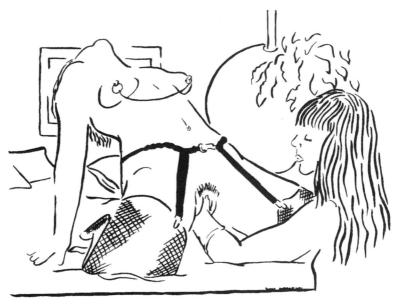

If that edge position is too limber for you, place your ass as close to the edge of the bed as possible. Grab a couple of chairs, and use the backs of them to prop your legs up – either under your knees or your calves – much like stirrups in your ob-gyn's office. The fister has excellent access to your cunt in this position, and you have your vulva within easy reach.

A sofa with a low-ish back makes a good fisting platform; the fistee sits on the back of the couch, leaning against the wall for support. The fister positions herself beneath the fistee, perpendicular to her. This is a great non-tiring position that affords both participants excellent control over the insertion process. Just be sure to put something down on the sofa to protect your furniture.

Having first-hand experience with fisting in a sling, I can say with much confidence that slings are yummy (please see the Reference section for slingy resources). A sling is a large squarish or rectangular piece of leather or canvas suspended from the ceiling by chain at each of the four corners. It resembles a hammock, only shorter. Attached by clips to the chains closest to your legs are loops that you put your feet through, which support your ankles. Some slings have neck and head supports built in; you can also have a friend stand behind you as a headrest (and an extra pair of free hands – the better to fondle you with, Dear Reader). Slings are available in a fairly wide range of materials and prices. If you can't afford to buy one, check out your local playspaces or dungeons, or look into making one yourself.

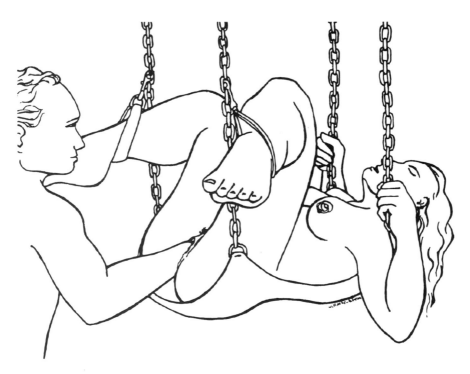

A sling is very comfortable. It conforms to your shape. It affords tremendous access to all of your body; lovers and assistants can get right up next to you on all sides for more tactile sensation, and you could even have someone beneath you, massaging or using a vibrator on your back through the sling. It feels incredible to have people on all sides; I love closing my eyes and just feeling what's being done, not being able to tell whose touch is doing what and where. The sensations pour over me like hot fudge over soft-serve ice cream; I lose myself in the melting delirium.

Your fister has a great view of and swell access to your cunt; with your legs spread up and out, you're comfortably wide open. The fister can pull up a chair, and will tire far less easily than in many other positions. Slings aren't exactly stationary objects, but they're perfectly safe and stable when mounted correctly. They add a wonderful dimension of moving, kinetic rhythm to fisting. If you're being fisted while lying on a bed or sitting on a kitchen counter, you can feel your fister gently moving back and forth while you remain relatively still. In a sling, you not only experience your fister's motions, you become a part of the motion. Your whole body participates in the rocking, swaying, tidal strokes.

My first fisting experience in a sling involved me as the fistee. I had people on all four sides of me, immersing me in fingers, kisses and lube. There was a mirror on the ceiling right above me (mylar, to be exact; it's cheaper, and won't shatter in an earthquake or fall on you and break into a million little shards) that gave me a great view of the proceedings, from a front-row seat. When I could manage to keep my eyes open, it was amazing to be able to watch what it was that was making my head swim. It was a blissfully memorable experience; of all of the positions in which I've experienced fisting, I must say that slings are my favorite way to go.

Variations

There's more than one way to experience fisting; you're limited only by your imagination and communication skills.

Don't hesitate to employ any toy that makes fisting a more pleasurable experience for you. Vibrators, dildos and butt plugs are just a few of the options available. A lover of mine enjoyed using a vibrator on her clit and having a finger or small plug in her ass while being fisted; she said that's when her orgasms were most intense. She loved the feeling of being completely filled and having all of her pleasure receptors tickled simultaneously. From the feel of her orgasms, I must say she had the right idea.

Many women enjoy having several kinds of stimuli going on at the same time. With your free hand, you could play with her clit, touch her all over (or at least as far as you can reach) or place a finger (gently, please, and with lots of lube on the glove) in her ass. Do *not* move a finger, a toy or a fist from her ass to her cunt without thoroughly washing it first with antibacterial soap and putting a fresh glove or condom over it; anal bacteria can cause serious infections in a vagina.

You can lick her where she likes to be licked, or kiss the insides of her thighs. Fisters often find themselves with their hands rather full; if your fister is a little busy with the process of making your head explode, then please, feel free to run your own hands over breast, neck, thigh or wherever your hands may pleasurably roam. Have an intimate dialogue with your own hands and body; let your fingers do the talking.

Over the years, I've had a little bit of sex. Of all the positions, people, toys, techniques and variations I've tried, the most amazing sexual experience I've ever had was when a lover and I fisted each other at the same time. It was a closed loop of sensation; we both came at the same time, and it was breathtaking to have my orgasm, have her inside me, be inside her, feel her orgasm, watch her orgasm, watch her watching my orgasm, watching her watching me watch her orgasm... it was one of those utterly magical moments where time really did stand still.

Some women enjoy having lots of flavors on their sexual menu. Our culture frowns on the idea, but it's entirely possible to have healthy sexual relationships with more than one person at a time (for more information on healthy nonmonogamy, check the reference section). Fisting can be done with more than two people in the room, either participating or watching. A friend of mine swears that being fisted while she's giving head and being fucked anally is a huge rush. I'm more than willing to take her word for it.

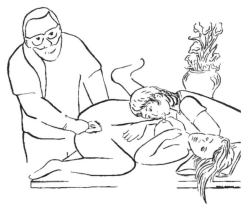

Another option for women who enjoy feeling very filled is to be fisted vaginally and anally at the same time. It helps if the ratio of fisters to fistees is 2:1 in this situation; if one fister tries to fist both orifices, she's likely to get a little short-handed, or his nose will inevitably begin to itch furiously. With two fisters, there's at least one hand free to reach for the lube, gloves, nose, or what-have-you.

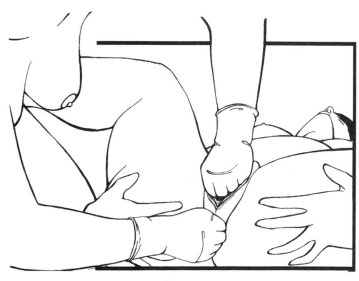

For a woman who likes to push her limits yet isn't interested in exploring anal fisting, having a fister dive in with both hands might be the answer. The same rules for inserting one fist applies to inserting two; the main difference would be that each hand would not be clenched into separate fists. If you do make it in with both hands, try clasping them together (pretend you're applauding, only don't pull your hands apart), or interlacing your fingers and pulling your hands close together that way.

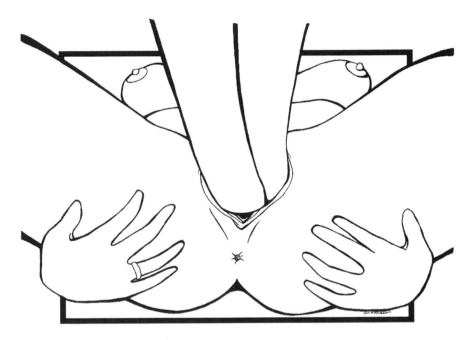

After my unpleasant experience with domestic terrorism, I spent six months in a wheelchair. I was in a full leg cast and a lot of pain, but I was able to discover that fisting while in a wheelchair is not only possible, but a very pleasant distraction to boot.

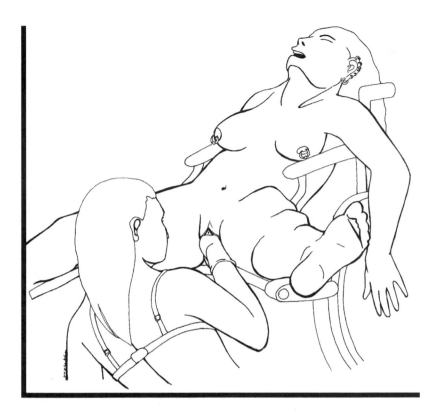

I have an acquaintance who lost his hand just above the wrist in a mill accident. Technically, I don't suppose it qualifies as fisting, but the morning after he's used his foreshortened appendage, his lover just shrugs her shoulders when asked what's up, smiles that smile, and says, "I'm stumped!"

A friend told me of a conversation she'd overheard at a gathering where fisting was being done. A few folks that hadn't seen fisting done before were looking on at a fisting; they assumed that the fister was an amputee and were lamenting the unfortunate person's appendage loss; they assumed that the poor fister was an amputee because, of course, one couldn't *possibly* get an entire hand in there!

If you are missing anywhere from a single digit to a whole hand to most of a forearm, you can still be a fister. Extra-large condoms will serve in lieu of gloves. Remember, though, that there is no narrow spot, like the wrist; the part that's inside her is going to be roughly the same diameter as the part the vaginal sphincter will be coping with and as the part of your arm that you can see. It might take a bit more working up to achieve that sort of a stretch, but lots of practice with dildos (start in the isn't-that-cute size range and work your way up to the ohmigawd model) will be helpful.

Holding hands

Fisting is a deeply moving experience for everyone involved. Don't plan on jumping out of bed or down off the kitchen counter to go do the grocery shopping or pick up your dry cleaning. Give yourselves plenty of time to come down and unwind. You're going to be really gooey afterwards; it's nice to have some warm water and towels by the sling or the sofa, with which to clean up so that you don't have to run to the bathroom. Snuggle. Kiss and touch. Talk about how it felt for you. Talk about what worked really well, what you'd like to have happen again; discuss gently and in non-accusatory terms what didn't work quite so well, what you'd like not to have happen again. Giggle. Doze off for a few minutes, and wake in each other's arms, noodley and smiling. Take a bath or shower together. Notice how your face feels from being sweet and dreamy. Say nothing. Caress and reassure. Compliment and share.

You may find yourself a little sore after having been fisted. It shouldn't be any worse than the way it feels after a particularly rousing and vigorous finger- or dick-fuck; the soreness shouldn't be more than a subtle, warm reminder of a very pleasant encounter. When I find myself a bit nether-tender after a good fisting, it brings a warm, delicate smile to my face – the kind of smile that makes other people wonder what I've been up to.

CONCLUSION

THE HAND⊕FF

Fisting is a miraculous experience. It is power, surrender, exchange and bliss. For me, it is a sacred rite; I don't allow anything but trust, lust and respect into my cunt. Fisting is a ritual; it requires so much of my attention that there just isn't room for me to be, do or think anything else. It is perhaps the most binding of sexual acts; at no other moment do I feel as close to another human being as at the moment when her fist becomes, if only for a brief while, an actual, physical part of me, or at the moment my fist in her cunt pulses in time to her essential rhythms as though I were one of her vital organs.

I hope you've found within these pages a guide to your own little slice of fisting heaven. I welcome your stories, suggestions, and questions; please feel free to send them in, care of Greenery Press.

⊕THER V⊕ICES
A cunt lovers' chorus

I've been blessed with the presence of many talented folks in my life; I've included here some of their voices, so that they can sing to you as joyfully as they sing to me. There aren't as many male voices as I had hoped to include, but the ones I do have are wonderful. Represented here are the voices of women, men, lesbians, not lesbians, sadomasochists, not sadomasochists, sexual adventurers who beat around bushes seeking new delights, and the sexually timid who quietly create their sexuality within their own walls. My heart is in my hand as I offer them my thanks for sharing with me, and as I offer to share them with you.

These first two pieces were written by my beloved faun, the first person with whom I shared fisting. She is missed, but her words are true as ever.

Daisy

I have felt this way before:
my body is rigid
and long
much longer than I remember it being.

slightly curved
definitely marked.

shades of green
color the startling moments
when
through this body
I have felt
the diffusing reactions of growth,
and inevitable moments
when my head
bursts wide open,
pushing out the timid, fragile center –

pieces

carefully enveloped
by arms and legs and
bodies of protecting petals;
limbs which once felt sturdy
now flimsy,
separated,
open.

faun

Smooth backslopes like ice

(on which my
fingers, nails,
skate
making perfect graceful
pirouettes and figures
and occasional

leaps)

start at the top.
the shoulder peak
where it's hard

(gathering speed breezing
descent to the soft curves
and swells of
her surface).

I'm scraping my breath
hot and hard
into this burning ice.
This

(neck
shoulder
side
hip
folds
cave)

reminds me
as my fingers tingle,
numbed by flesh
immersed in ripples,
clenched tight,
that I want to be
burned.

I hang my dripping
skates to dry.
Remember my longing
to break through
the ice
and immerse my
self in
the swift currents,
an under water
cavern,
where I can
hear
ice
cracking
above me and my
breath comes thick hard quick.

I feel I am inside
the heartbeat
of everything.

faun

Jain is a dear friend, with whom I have much in common. She has quite a way with words; I'm sure you'll enjoy her as much as I do.

My first fisting experience was kinda surprising. My girlfriend and I had been apart for a week while she was off on a business trip, and I didn't masturbate the whole time she was gone; I wanted to save up all my sexual energy to give to her when she got back.

I picked her up at the airport, and took her home. I made her one of her favorite meals, and had set up the bathroom with candles, incense, and her special bath stuff. After I fed her dinner with my fingers, I drew her bath, and gently cleansed her tired skin, working out the muscle knots she always gets from sleeping in a strange bed. I poured her out of the tub, and into bed. She dozed for a while, while I petted and kissed her all over. Slowly, she began to come 'round, responding sweetly to me. The air smelled like cunt, girljuice and heat.

My favorite way to orgasm is with her fingers inside me, while I use a vibrator on my clit. Two of her fingers in me wasn't enough. Neither was three, nor four. I just kept telling her, "more, more!" and she kept feeding me with her fingers, until I'd eaten her whole hand. I'll never forget that moment, after her whole had slid into me and curled into a ball. We both just froze, staring into each other's eyes. I'd never felt so close, so closely linked to anyone before. It was miraculous, that moment.

It musta been my week's celibacy that left me wet enough with my own juice to eat her up like that; we've been fisting ever since that first time, but we always use lots of extra lube. Doesn't matter to me. I'd use anything – spit, cum, 'jac, whatever – if I thought it would get her fist in me slicker and quicker. I'm always hungry now.

Jain d'Eaux

Dossie is one of my favorite writers, and a sexual pioneer to whom I owe a great debt. Check your local sexuality library and see if you find any of her other fine poems haunting the pages of other books, written under the name Scarlet Woman. Happy hunting!

ROLL ME OVER & MAKE ME A ROSE

This morning you amazed me
    in my sleeping you
        moved into my dream
            with fast hands
Sure hands on my sleepy ass
    on my clit
        in my cunt
Engorging
Under fast hands alarmed
    into instant arousal I
Gasp
    sliding under covers
You grasping me I could be unsure
    of my turn-on
        before arising
But riding your command I am
    carried away

You move in faster than
    I can decide
        to trust you
I hang on to you
    galloping me over waves
        pounding scarlet
My brain is asleep and my
Cunt is a rose
    riding your hand

Roll me over in the morning
    lover
    and make me a rose

Dossie Easton

Catherine is another one of my favorite authors, and is a favored playmate. We haven't shared fisting with each other yet, but she's agreed to share this fisting story with all of us:

As a sex educator, I'm always telling people that any part of the body can be an erogenous zone – so it's surprising and a bit embarrassing that it took me as long as it did to figure out that my hand could be as erotically sensitive as my nipples or my genitals.

One of the first times I fisted my girlfriend was at a sex party. She was sitting in a semi-reclining position on a doctor's examining table, with her knees in the stirrups. I was playing with her tits and clit with my left hand while I put two fingers, then three, then four into her with my right hand. As she opened up to me, pushing herself downward against me, I felt my hand push past the tight part at the outside and up into her. I'm always amazed at how hot it is in there. Her cunt completely surrounded my hand, with a not-so-gentle pressure pushing in from all directions at once, soft and squishy on the surface yet with hard muscles pulsing and quivering behind it.

I began gently moving my hand back and forth, letting the muscles at the base of my palm pull backwards against the muscles at the mouth of her vagina, then releasing the pressure, establishing a heartbeat-like rhythm in time to her moans and cries. I found myself rocking back and forth with the rhythm, almost dancing, feeling the beat sway up through my knees and hips. I was pressing the front of my cunt against the edge of the table. She saw what I was doing and pushed her foot toward me, inviting me to hump it. I got it between my legs and began to rub myself against it. Feeling my arousal fed hers - she began to come, her inner muscles almost crushing the bones in my hand with their power and heat. That was all it took. I felt the blood surging up into my face and chest as my whole body began to quiver, then I cried out and came, pressing myself toward her body and feeling my hand being squeezed, squeezed, squeezed as she smiled up at me.

That was the first time I ever came while fisting someone – but not the last.

Catherine A. Liszt

Not all first fists make it all the way in. This piece was given me by my loony Knight in slightly dented armor; I love him dearly. He excels at the business of talking people down from staggering mental precipices, and has a childlike joy in discovering sexuality in its many forms. He was a big help to me during the writing of this book, and perhaps his tale will be of assistance to you.

My first experience of the fisting nature was reaching my fingers inside of my partner's cunt and, with childlike curiosity feeling all the different parts (finding the "G-spot" was interesting). I actually became further interested by watching a couple at a party; a woman, decked head to toe with piercings, was on top of another woman... working her partner's cunt open enough to allow her hand, while her partner looked, not in pain, yet obviously having an incredibly intense experience. At that point I decided "I want to do this."

My experiences since have been brief. My partner at the time had been interested in fisting for some time so negotiating a lesson wasn't difficult. We played and I started working her cunt open to the point I could get all my fingers inside, meanwhile feeling her exude intense energies similar to those I remember from the experience I witnessed at the party before. I was exhilarated by the feeling of power of being there. We could only get so far, though; the bridge of my hand was too wide, and I couldn't get her to loosen up any further. Being it was a first time, we wound back down and considered trying again another time.

Derek

Fisting isn't for everyone. There are certain physical conditions that make a woman an unlikely fistee; there are many more mental and emotional factors that can make an act as intimate and potent as fisting an unpleasantly traumatic experience. Molestation as a child, mental, emotional or sexual abuse by a family member or partner and rape are only a few of the things that can put a woman in a fisting-fearful place. This piece grieves me no end; it saddens and enrages me when parts of a woman's sexuality are taken away from her without her consent. Whatever the reason that makes it so, fisting just isn't an option for some women.

I've had two experiences with fisting, both negative, really. Thinking about this, I'm not sure whether it was the actual experience or whether it was just the woman I got involved with, or whether it was my own sexual issues... probably a little of all of them.

I was seventeen during my first experience with fisting and, having only been acquainted with simple, gentle digital arousal, I was apprehensive when my lover suddenly tried to work herself into me. I felt it overly intimate and prying, as if she was yanking at something. Being that I was so young, and as she was an older woman, I felt somewhat intimidated and simply went along with it, thinking I might enjoy the experience after all... but I didn't.

The second time happened only recently, over ten years from the first time. I had been with a few other women since, and knew what I expected in the way of sexual enjoyment. My lover (to her credit) let me know what she wanted and asked me for consent. I agreed because I trusted her and thought that the experience would be more positive than before. Again, I found the experience uncomfortable and not arousing in the least. I don't like the prying of it, the probing of it, and, quite frankly, I don't really like someone having that much access to my innards.

Lynne G

I haven't yet had the pleasure of meeting Connie, but this poem makes me think I'd like to...

HOMO HOMINIDS GET IT ON IN THE ZOO PARKING LOT

after a day
admiring hairy
and hairless genitals
and breathing sex charged air,
we evolved
from primitive grunts
to modern sex-talk.
    softer harder
    wait ok inside
    mmmuhhfuck me now
    yesaaughgiveittome.
one curls her cunt
around the other's hand
between unhs and ahms,
exposed like the chimp's
wide wild teeth
and hairy underarms.
we grunt and push in or down
smack our lips
and fingers clean
of snatch juice
reminiscent of
banana-pineapple cream.

Connie Meredith

Yew is a student single mom-type woman who is a wonderfully peaceful presence. She's normally so calm and understated about things, that when she uses an expletive, it's taken very seriously, and for good reason. She had this to say about the fisting experience: "Whether your fisting preference is a slow, screwing motion or an intense pounding, be prepared for the desire to be uncontainable."

Uncontainable

reach through my valley.
    feel my mountains widen.
add the rest, as I beg for more.
The screams escape my lips.
As the river rises and reaches its crest,
    take a deep breath and ride with me.
the current sweeps us to a
    blissful place.

Yew

When I asked my darling KT for a blurb about fisting, she made a sad face and said, "I'd love to, but I haven't tried it yet." I assured her that a fistment of her imagination would be a wonderful addition. I was honored to be the object of her fantasy; I hope to return the favor of her creation by helping to make it a reality.

It begins gradually. Pretty soon your finger searches for the source of the wet pool of my juices. As you explore another finger joins the first, and opens up a cavern inside of me. Two fingers are no longer enough and another and then another join in. As my pelvis rocks and the cave grows more spacious, you continue to explore and excite until finally your hand is entirely inside of me. You rock and dance with me, choreographing my excitement with your fist. We share a space inside that we created together. As you build me higher and higher, I let go into your guidance until finally distinctions of self and other, before and after, inside and outside dissolve into exuberant exhaustion. Sometime later I surface, aware of your hand resting against my pussy, your body cradling mine, separate and satisfied.

KT

Kat is a very longtime friend and playmate. She's a recovered bottom-nee Top cum switch who wears many hats in the vanilla world and yet still has time to frequent various Internet chat rooms, and be a lover, mother, and, recently, grandmother of two. We've helped each other grow over many an obstacle, and she's always there with words like these to offer anyone who has a question that seeks its answer, or a fear that needs to be conquered (she doesn't know it, but she's one of my favorite people in the whole universe). She's been through many levels of DanteLand, and is a fire in the night for those who need warmth and light. Here, she sheds some illumination on overcoming physical challenges.

I had an abdominal full hysterectomy... they removed uterus, cervix, and connecting tissues, including the fallopian tubes, left the ovaries. My healing was outstanding... well above the norm. I was driving in four days, working in six, after the surgery. The instructions were "no sex" for six weeks... but by three I was so horny, I convinced my partner to make love to me... very wary, she agreed... but would insert only one finger, just barely inside the vagina, and concentrated her efforts on my clit. It was brief, and mild, as my orgasms went at the time, I think I might have been afraid of tearing things up inside. I was a bit tender for about half an hour, but no other deleterious effects.

I called the doctor the next day, and had the nurse confirm that no sex actually meant no penetration, and happily enough waited out the next three weeks with clitoral orgasms only.

The first time S. was brave enough to use a couple fingers in me, I remember being thrilled at the fullness again... but we both noticed in a heartbeat (and I've confirmed from the fister side, with D.) that the pathway and accommodations were rather limited... stands to reason when you cut out the cervix, and sew up the end of the vagina, you're going to lose some of the space available. We took it slowly, as any couple would have at first, and allowed the tissue of the vagina some time to get used to stretching again. I should mention that again, I was probably ahead of the game... it probably took a whole three weeks from two fingers to S.'s fist... but she did have lovely slender hands, and that helped facilitate an earlier return than might have been possible if my partner had larger hands like mine.

My biggest disappointment with the whole thing, and that would be the same whether I was straight or gay, is that the root of my orgasms used to be at my uterus... its contractions seemed to rule the entire body at climax. Imagine the horror and feeling of loss, knowing that something is supposed to be happening... and you can't feel it, see it... can't make it over the top of the wall. Everything in my abdomen pulled towards the uterus, to help with the push... but in the center of it all... there was a hollow. That realization left me devastated at first.

Eventually, all the body parts managed to cope with the absence, and the orgasms are satisfactory again, even enjoyable... but I still know something's missing. Obviously, I can't let changes stop me though, from enjoying the rest of the experience.

Though my uterus may be history, there's no doubt that the muscles have completely recovered, it's rather nice to be able not only to push out an invading fist, but to imprison it, hold it captive, and caress it, as well. It did not hurt more than it should have... didn't realize it should have hurt at all, beyond the minor stretching of the bones to accommodate the width of a hand... D's hands are so small that with lube, I can often accommodate her before I've had a single orgasm, and she takes a particular delight in removing and re-inserting with every stroke at times, something you and I would find almost impossible to do.

Kathleen Perrault

This is a very fine piece from a cyberpal of mine who lives in Canada. She's a bottom, she walks on four wheels instead of two legs, has an amazing sense of humor and an incredible sense of perspective. When I asked her for a donation of words for this book, I had no idea that she'd send me something that would knock the wind out of me like this piece did.

In The Moment

I am skin
   on wood
      on leather
         on metal
I am rough smooth hard soft
 thrust hit   pound
   inhale
      exhale
I am not here
   there
I am not weelz
   not cath
      not me
I am sub empty
I am filled
   full
      fulfilled
I am not mine
   give offer
      take accept allow
I am not free
      I am free
I am sharp gasp past
   last
      first
I am yes
      I am not no
I am breath
I am scream
   I am scream

inhale
I am stroke count count count
   count
    lose count
      I am scream
        exhale
          I am scream
I am fingers onside inside
I am wait
   wait
I am not now
   wait
   wait
I am   yes   now
I am not ending
   forever never
   ever for
I am
   I am
      I am

weelz

A denizen of the IRC, this Dragon Lady has claws as sharp as her wits, and a touch as gentle as she is fierce. I always enjoy collaborating with her, and am terribly pleased to include her voice here.

Fisting – gloving your hand in your lover's vulnerability, capturing the helix of power, being held immobile by the release   of emotion. It is the Ultimate feeling of possessing and being possessed, feeling your lover's pussy clench and contract and then spasm so tightly around your hand that it goes numb or feels like it's about to break your wrist. Fisting – reaching out of soul into soul, akin to plugging yourself into the light socket of their entirety. Definitely a favorite activity!

SilvrDrgn

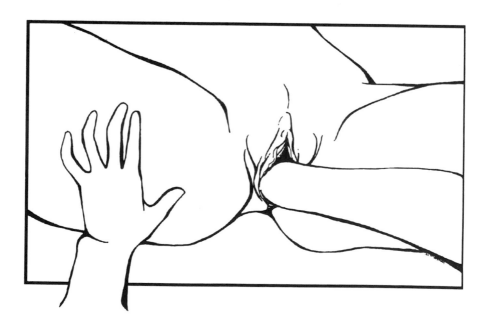

This gentleman friend works with his hands for a living. He and his wife learned a lot about fisting by trial and error; hopefully his advice will spare you most of the trial and all of the error.

Fisting can be a very erotic experience, but if you work with your hands all day, beware! Those calloused hands that she finds so attractive when snuggling on the couch will seem a lot less so when they encounter the tender tissues of her vagina. If you work with volatile solvents, you've even more of a problem. Methyl ethyl ketone, lacquer thinner, toluene, trichlorethylene, Berryman's B-9 and all other parts cleaners, mineral spirits (paint thinner), acetone, and alcohol all penetrate the skin very easily. Even diesel and gasoline are easily absorbed. All will, at the very least, irritate the vagina. At worst, your lover could end up in the hospital with some very serious vaginal problems.

A good rule of thumb to follow is: If you can smell it on your hands, sufficient quantity of the solvent exists in the pores of your skin to be a potential hazard. Fortunately, both hard callouses and solvents can be dealt with very easily. Soak your hands in Hexol. It works best in hot water – the hotter the better. A few minutes of soaking will work the solvent out of your skin and soften those nasty callouses. Finish by washing your hands thoroughly with a good, mild soap.

This final step is very important! Hexol can be an irritant too, and its disinfecting properties will kill bacteria that the vagina needs to remain healthy. So wash thoroughly – and then enjoy!

MJ Matson

The next two stories are from Jaymes and Susan, close friends of my publisher. They are, I'm told, an unusual and wonderful couple.

O had been in an accident and suffered from recurrent muscle spasms. She was off work on disability, taking Valium and Flexoril, when I met her. We started having sex, and I turned her on to kink. She easily turned on to fisting, and we would spend hours with my hand in her cunny. About this time I had to go home for a month to take care of my father. When I returned, O's condition had improved and she had stopped taking the drugs. We got together to play and discovered to her despair that it was almost impossible for me to get my hand in her. I then realized it had been the muscle relaxants that had allowed us to easily enjoy fisting. This is not to endorse drugged play, but to be aware of the side effects of drugs.

P is an interesting submissive. It is difficult for her to allow herself to be pleasured while in a submissive state. She is the only person I know who has orgasms being mouth fucked. To enable her to be fisted, I have to direct her to impale herself on my hand. I order her onto her hands and knees with her ass towards me. I lube and place the beak of my hand against and just inside her lips. Then I command her to back up until she can go no farther. She will only move if I direct her to. She can only come if she is whacked with my other hand, or a crop.

Q was always compulsively cleaning up when she stayed over. One morning I decided to torment her by fingering her 'gina while she washed breakfast dishes. It wasn't long before the fingers became a fist, and we both discovered that leaning her over the kitchen sink was the easiest way to hand fuck her. Q finished washing the dishes with my hand in her. She was always a good girl.

The first time I fisted R happend one morning before she even opened her eyes. We had been trying to get my hand in her for several weeks, but it just seemed as though it couldn't be done. While she was willing, her vagina wasn't. One morning, with no intention of fisting her, I planned to wake her with lubed and gloved fingers. One and then two and then three fingers slid easily in. It was almost by accident that the rest of my hand fell into her sleeping vagina. When R woke up a minute later with my hand inside her, this most submissive young woman had a wild fire in her eyes. I thought she was royally pissed off at me. I asked her if she wanted me to take it out. She replied, "If you do, I'll kill you." Later, I asked her if she could come – she said she didn't want to; it wouldn't feel as good.

I believe it was the second time that S and I played in this manner, that I noticed that my watch was about to disappear into her vagina. Being an eminently practical man, I didn't want my watch to get smoochy, so I said matter-of-factly to her, "Could you please take my watch off?" This totally cracked her up, and took her right out of the headspace she was in. What had before been a soft, pliant pussy was now locked tighter than an iron maiden. There was no way I could get my hand out without really hurting her. It took us several minutes to restore the former ambiance to comfortably proceed.

Jaymes Easton

And one of the same stories from the other point of view...

One morning, while still asleep, I heard Jaymes' voice: "Get on your back! Open your legs!" You know, terms of endearment. Well, the next thing I knew, for the first time in my life, I was being fisted – professionally! and very personally. Then Jaymes said, "Look... look at my arm, and where it is." I wasn't sure that my brain could comprehend what my eyes were looking at – whose arm and hand WAS that? and in WHOSE pussy? WOW! Then he had me get off the bed and WALK over to the full-length mirror so I could get a really good look at this phenomenon. Talk about an out-of-body experience! (or is that an "into-body" experience?) Needless to say, that image in the mirror remains burned upon one of the pages in the memory book of my mind.

Susan S.

This isn't exactly an "other" voice, but I couldn't resist....

Invitation

I know you ain't no
prettie grrrrl

and I don't care
and I don't care that
you don't care that
I don't care

shut up and dance

I want you to
grab holda my
cunt
with your whole hand
like you gotta holda my
heart with your
broken   words

and then
cuz we're both fuct up
you gotta write a song

about that time when
you grabbed my neck
and fingered my frets
and filled the hole in the hourglass
with singing sound

so I can smile when I hear it
cuz it's about me
and fiva yer geetar pickin fingers
rolled inta one big
crescendo

cummawn, Ani
I dare ya

E⌀ACULATI⊕N
and fisting

I had a lover who was ejaculative. I'd always been a little jealous of her; when she came, it was with a tide of juice that amazed and aroused me. I just figured, since I hadn't ever ejaculated, that I was one of those women who simply couldn't do it. I wasn't non-ejaculative because my orgasms weren't intense enough; I had no complaints. But I always envied my lovers who could 'jac. I saw how consuming their orgasms were. I know how incredibly turned on I got by watching, feeling and tasting their orgasms, watching her juice run down my arm or feeling it bathe my face. It wasn't until I got fisted that I discovered how to 'jac.

All of my life, I had pulled my orgasms inward. I had a severe case of incontinence anxiety (I was terrified that I was going to pee uncontrollably when I came); when I came, I clenched all my muscles instead of "pushing" them. I did some reading and watched a video (see the reference section for more info on teaching yourself how to 'jac), and found out that female ejaculation has been around as long as females have, that female ejaculate is of a different chemical composition that urine, and that, when I felt an urge at orgasm similar to the feeling of a pressing need to urinate, it was ejaculation, not urination, that was wanting to happen.

With a fist inside me, I was able to let go of that retentive muscle contraction. My lover's fist gave me something to push against. Between having something to push against and the amazing intensity of a fisting orgasm, before I knew it, I was soaking the sheets.

A fist occupies pretty much every centimeter of available space in a cunt. Fisting applies pressure to the urethral sponge in a way that no other sexual act does. Because of this pressure, a woman who has never ejaculated before may surprise both herself and her partner with the forceful expulsion of fluids. Fisting taught me that I could ejaculate; I've since taught myself how to do it "on command." It can be controlled; I can keep it from happening if I want to. The thing is that ejaculating makes my orgasms feel much more consuming, much more complete; because I've learned the muscle control essential to easy fisting, I can choose what type of orgasm I want from any sexual encounter (even if it's just me encoutering myself).

APPENDIX II

BE SELFIST,
and go fuck yourself

If you decide you're limber and adventurous enough to try fisting yourself, you can easily adapt the how-to information in this book to a singular approach, and combine that information with the tips in this section.

Recline on your sofa or comfy chair with your legs and feet propped up. Make certain that you won't be rudely interrupted in the middle of things; lock doors, turn phones off, and have plenty of time to yourself. Sudden muscular jolts due to a surprise won't feel good to your fist or your cunt, and extracting your fist from your cunt (or anyone else's, for

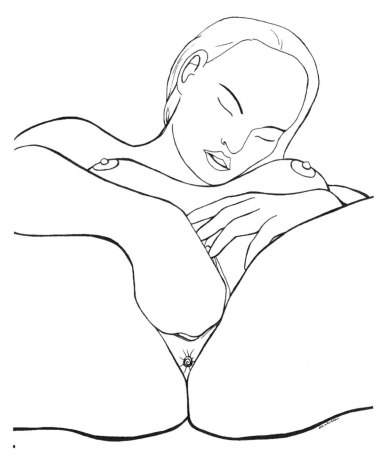

that matter) shouldn't be done abruptly. You'll probably want to masturbate (with or without a vibrator) to warm up. Go slow. The advantage to fisting yourself is that you won't need to worry about your lover going too hard, fast or far.

A website I visited while looking for electronic resource references said that if you fist yourself, you could possibly break your fingers or wrist (because of the intense muscle contractions of orgasm), or crush your clitoris. That is erroneous information. The chance of those things happening is about a bazillion to .0000000000000001. If you're fisting yourself, you're wearing both a fister's as well as a fistee's hat; you won't just feel what it feels like to be a fistee, but you'll also (hopefully) find yourself to be a gentle and responsive fister. All of the input you'll get from trying to fist yourself, whether you make it all the way in or not, could be very useful when discussing fisting with a partner.

DRUGS & FISTING
When the incredible act of fisting becomes a really bad idea

Any type of sex can be dangerous if it is not consensual, or if it's done incorrectly. This is decidedly true of fisting. Fisting has a pretty bad rap; many people help to perpetuate this misinformation. Fisting is no more dangerous that any other sex act *if it's done correctly*.

Another item that has helped to keep fisting in the category of no-no is what can happen if it's done wrong. I was able to locate one instance of a vaginal fisting-related death in medical journals. In that instance, the woman died from hemorrhage and internal bleeding. Had she been able to seek medical attention immediately after the injury, she would probably have lived. The damage went undetected. The victim was a runaway minor female, fisted, passed out from a combination of methamphetamines and alcohol, and left to die in a cheap motel room. Yes, fisting could kill you, under certain very extreme and completely preventable conditions.

It's been argued that a little alcohol or marijuana can encourage relaxation and reduce inhibitions, thereby helping one try something new, different or even a little scary. People do things they might not ordinarily do when they're drunk or stoned. Some drugs, especially psychotropics (drugs that significantly alter one's perceptions of reality), are said to add new dimensions of wonder and intensity to sexual encounters. Methamphetamines are supposed to lend one a clarity of perception that may render sexual acts more intense and vivid. Be all this as it may, if a fist is what one plans to place in a cunt, then there is absolutely no room for drugs – and I include alcohol under that heading. Prescription medications should also be used with care; if you're taking any pain medication, for instance, it's advisable to abstain from it for a few hours prior to and for the duration of your fisting encounter.

A fistee can not afford to lose her sense of what's going on in her body; if pain impulses are dulled, she may not know it if something gets damaged. A fister can not afford to have impaired judgment; an overzealous fister can do irreparable – sometimes fatal – damage to the fistee. Any drug that gives you "cottonmouth," such as antihistamines and marijuana, can greatly reduce natural vaginal secretions, and cause rigidity in the mucous membranes and vaginal tissue, making fisting a risky proposition.

Fisting creates such overwhelmingly psychological effects in its own right that taking a drug is usually a waste of the intoxicant intended to enhance the experience. Fisting does not need to be chemically enhanced in order to make it an incredibly intense experience. Never fist anyone who is intoxicated; you could unintentionally injure her, and she'd never know it. Never allow yourself to be fisted by an intoxicated individual; anything less than a conscientious, cautious fister could do you serious bodily harm. If someone is too intoxicated to drive your car, they have no business placing their hand in your cunt. If you are too intoxicated to drive your car, you have no business letting someone in your cunt. Cunts, fists and drugs of any sort *do not* mix.

TR⊕UBLE~
shooting

Done correctly, fisting is no more or less risky than any other form of sexual interaction. As with any other sex act, however, it's possible for something to go wrong.

Medical intervention becomes wise and necessary if:

* you have some spotting that lasts for more than twenty-four hours after having been fisted;

* you can see a visible vaginal or labial tear or rupture;

* you have persistent pain above and beyond the level of minor post-fucking soreness;

* you experience heavy bleeding, with or without clots, if it's not close enough to your period to be menstrual blood;

* you run a high fever;

* your wrist swells, is quite sore, and doesn't want to move the way it usually does.

If these or any other symptoms not common to you appear, seek medical attention *immediately*. Now is not the time to be modest – tell your physician what you've been up to, and show her this book if she's not familiar with the practice. You won't get the best treatment if your doctor doesn't know what's going on.

RES⊕URCE
Guide

For more information about vaginal fisting:

The Good Vibrations Guide to Sex
Cathy Winks and Anne Semans
Cleis Press, Pittsburgh, PA

"Mama's Got A Squeezebox, Daddy Never Sleeps At Night"
an article by Pat Califia appearing in **Sandmutopia Guardian**, Issue 15,
Feb. '94, pps. 18-21

http://weber.u.washington.edu/~sfpse/safesex.html
a website maintained by Society for Human Sexuality, University of
Washington, Seattle, WA

Some good videos that show fisting and/or female ejaculation:

How to Female Ejaculate (with Carol Queen, Fanny Fatale, Shannon Bell)
1992
Fatale Video, San Francisco

Private Pleasures and Shadows
1995
Fatale Video, San Francisco

Sluts and Goddesses (with Annie Sprinkle, Scarlet Harlot, Trash)
1992
Beatty/Sprinkle

For information about anal fisting:

Trust: The Handbook
Bert Herrman
Alamo Square Press, San Francisco

Anal Pleasure and Health: A Guide for Men and Women
Jack Morin, Ph.D.
Yes Press, San Francisco

For general information about female genitals and female sexuality:

A New View of a Woman's Body
The Federation of Feminist Women's Health Centers
Feminist Press
West Hollywood, CA

The New Our Bodies, Ourselves: A Book By and For Women
The Boston Women's Health Book Collective
A Touchstone Book, Simon and Schuster, New York

The Cunt Coloring Book
Tee Corinne
Last Gasp Books, San Francisco

For good insights about the nature of sexual arousal and how to get more of it:

Exhibitionism for the Shy
Carol Queen
Down There Press, San Francisco

The Erotic Mind
Jack Morin, Ph.D.
Perennial, New York

For information about nontraditional relationship structures:

The Ethical Slut: A Guide to Infinite Sexual Possibilities
Dossie Easton & Catherine A. Liszt
Greenery Press, San Francisco

Polyamory: The New Love Without Limits
Dr. Deborah M. Anapol
IntiNet Resource Center, San Rafael, CA

For information about S/M and related sexualities:

SM 101: A Realistic Introduction
Jay Wiseman
Greenery Press, San Francisco

Screw The Roses, Send Me The Thorns
Philip Miller & Molly Devon
Mystic Rose Books, Fairfield, CT

Sensuous Magic
Pat Califia
Masquerade Books, NY

Safe, Sane, Consensual... And Fun
John Warren
Diversified Services, Brighton, MA

Learning the Ropes
Race Bannon
Daedalus Press, San Francisco

The Bottoming Book: Or, How To Get Terrible Things Done To You By Wonderful People and **The Topping Book: Or, Getting Good At Being Bad**
Dossie Easton & Catherine A. Liszt
Greenery Press, San Francisco

For safer sex information:

The Complete Guide to Safer Sex
Institute for Advanced Study of Human Sexuality
San Francisco, CA

Condom Educator's Guide, Version Two
Daniel Bao and Beowulf Thorne
Condom Resource Center, Oakland, CA

National AIDS Hotline
(800) 342-AIDS

National STD Hotline
(800) 227-8922

For help in finding a fisting-positive physician, therapist or other professional:

Kink-Aware Professionals
c/o Race Bannon
584 Castro St. #518
San Francisco, CA 94114-2500
http://www.bannon.com/~race/kap

For help with domestic abuse:

National Domestic Violence Hotline
(800) 799-SAFE

For general sexuality information:

San Francisco Sex Information
(415) 989-7374
Free, anonymous, nonjudgmental sex information and referrals; open weekdays from 3 p.m. to 9 p.m. Pacific time

The Black Book
P.O. Box 31155
San Francisco, CA   94131-0155
A comprehensive national guide to sexuality clubs, stores, publications and other resources

IF YOU LIKED *THE SEXUALLY DOMINANT WOMAN,*
YOU MIGHT ENJOY:

BDSM & KINK

The Bottoming Book: Or, How To Get Terrible Things Done To You By Wonderful People
D. Easton & C.A. Liszt, ill. Fish $11.95

The Compleat Spanker
Lady Green $11.95

Jay Wiseman's Erotic Bondage Handbook
Jay Wiseman $15.95

Juice: Electricity for Pleasure and Pain
"Uncle Abdul" $11.95

KinkyCrafts: 99 Do-It-Yourself S/M Toys
Lady Green with Jaymes Easton $15.95

The Loving Dominant
John Warren $15.95

Miss Abernathy's Concise Slave Training Manual
Christina Abernathy $11.95

The Mistress Manual
Mistress Lorelei $15.95

SM 101: A Realistic Introduction
Jay Wiseman $24.95

The Topping Book: Or, Getting Good At Being Bad
D. Easton & C.A. Liszt, ill. Fish $11.95

Training With Miss Abernathy: A Workbook for Erotic Slaves and Their Owners
Christina Abernathy $11.95

GENERAL SEXUALITY

Big Big Love: A Sourcebook on Sex for People of Size and Those Who Love Them
Hanne Blank $15.95

The Ethical Slut: A Guide to Infinite Sexual Possibilities
Dossie Easton & Catherine A. Liszt $15.95

A Hand in the Bush: The Fine Art of Vaginal Fisting
Deborah Addington $11.95

Health Care Without Shame: A Handbook for the Sexually Diverse &Their Caregivers
Charles Moser, Ph.D., M.D. $11.95

Sex Toy Tricks: More than 125 Ways to Accessorize Good Sex
Jay Wiseman $11.95

The Strap-On Book
A.H. Dion, illustrated by Donna Barr $11.95

Supermarket Tricks: More than 125 Ways to Improvise Good Sex
Jay Wiseman $11.95

Tricks: More than 125 Ways to Make Good Sex Better
Jay Wiseman $11.95

Tricks 2: Another 125 Ways to Make Good Sex Better
Jay Wiseman $11.95

FICTION FROM GRASS STAIN PRESS

The 43rd Mistress: A Sensual Odyssey
Grant Antrews $11.95

Haughty Spirit
Sharon Green $11.95

Justice and Other Short Erotic Tales
Tammy Jo Eckhart $11.95

Murder At Roissy
John Warren $11.95

Please include $3 for first book and $1 for each additional book with your order to cover shipping and handling costs, plus $10 for overseas orders. VISA/MC accepted. Order from:

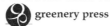 greenery press

1447 Park Ave., Emeryville, CA 94608
toll-free: 888/944-4434   http://www.bigrock.com/~greenery